The Art of Intercession

Handbook on How To Intercede

The Art of Intercession

Handbook on How To Intercede

Kenneth E. Hagin

Unless otherwise indicated, all Scripture quotations in this volume are from the *King James Version* of the Bible.
Scripture quotations indentified as *Amplified* are from *The Amplified Bible.*

Second Edition
First Printing 1987

ISBN 0-89276-511-9

In the U.S. write:
Kenneth Hagin Ministries
P.O. Box 50126
Tulsa, OK 74150-0126

In Canada write:
Kenneth Hagin Ministries
P.O. Box 335
Islington (Toronto), Ontario
Canada, M9A 4X3

BOOKS BY KENNETH E. HAGIN

The Gifts and Calling of God
Signs of the Times
Learning To Flow With the Spirit of God
The Glory of God
Hear and Be Healed
New Thresholds of Faith
*Prevailing Prayer to Peace
Concerning Spiritual Gifts
Bible Faith Study Course
Bible Prayer Study Course
The Holy Spirit and His Gifts
*The Ministry Gifts (Study Guide)
Seven Things You Should Know About Divine Healing
El Shaddai
Zoe: The God-Kind of Life
A Commonsense Guide to Fasting
Must Christians Suffer?
The Woman Question
The Believer's Authority
Ministering to Your Family
How You Can Be Led by the Spirit of God
What To Do When Faith Seems Weak and Victory Lost
The Name of Jesus
The Art of Intercession
Growing Up, Spiritually
Bodily Healing and the Atonement
Exceedingly Growing Faith
Understanding the Anointing
I Believe in Visions
Understanding How To Fight the Good Fight of Faith

BOOKS BY KENNETH HAGIN JR.

*Man's Impossibility — God's Possibility
Because of Jesus
The Key to the Supernatural
*Faith Worketh by Love
Blueprint for Building Strong Faith
*Seven Hindrances to Healing
*The Past Tense of God's Word
Healing: A Forever-Settled Subject
How To Make the Dream God Gave You Come True
Faith Takes Back What the Devil's Stolen
"The Prison Door Is Open — What Are You Still Doing Inside?"
Itching Ears
Where Do We Go From Here?
How To Be a Success in Life
Get Acquainted With God
Showdown With the Devil
Unforgiveness
The Answer for Oppression
Is Your Miracle Passing You By?
Commanding Power
The Life of Obedience
Ministering to the Brokenhearted

*These titles are also available in Spanish. Information about other foreign translations of several of the above titles (i.e., Dutch, Finnish, French, German, Indonesian, Polish, Russian, Swahili, and Swedish) may be obtained by writing to: Kenneth Hagin Ministries, P.O. Box 50126, Tulsa, Oklahoma 74150-0126.

Contents

Acknowledgment

Reverend Wilford H. Reidt of Kennewick, Washington, is an outstanding Bible teacher. Wilford's wife, Gertrude, is the daughter of John G. Lake, well-known apostle of faith in the early days of this century. Both Wilford and Gertrude are long-time intercessors, greatly used by God in this special ministry.

Wilford's teachings on the subject reveal a depth of knowledge only a real intercessor of some years' standing could teach. I was so impressed with his study outline and comments on the subject of intercession that I asked his permission to use it in this book to the glory of God. For we believe that God will use this book to raise up and train a great group of intercessors who will be at the forefront of the work of the Lord in these last days. Brother Reidt gave us permission and his remarks are set out in recognizable type.

Chapter 1

Why Pray?

Years ago I read a statement John Wesley made and it stayed with me. Wesley said, *"It seems God is limited by our prayer life—that He can do nothing for humanity unless someone asks Him."*

A while later, in 1949, I was reading after another writer who made that same statement. But this fellow added, *"Why this is, I do not know."*

"Why doesn't he know?" I asked. Then I found out I didn't know either.

Yet if Wesley's statement is correct—and it seems to be as you read through the Bible—then we who are to pray should know more about it.

I began to examine the Bible to find out why, if God wants to do something for humanity, He cannot unless somebody asks Him. I found the answer through study of God's Word.

You see, though some people have built up "spiritual air castles" that God is running everything in this world, He is not.

During the Vietnam War a nationally syndicated newspaper columnist began one column by stating that he was not a Christian. He said that he was not an atheist because the atheist says there is no God.

"I suppose you would classify me an agnostic," he wrote. "The agnostic says there may be a God, but if there is, I don't know it. Actually, I am prone to believe there is a Supreme Being. I do not believe that everything here just happened. I believe there is a Creator somewhere.

"But I have never read the Bible. I do not attend church. One reason I don't is that what the Christians say about God doesn't agree with what I think a Creator should be, nor with what I can see of Him in nature.

"Even ministers say, 'God has everything under control. He's running everything.'

"Well, if He is, He sure has things in a mess. People are killing each other. Little children are dying. Little children are hungry. Women are suffering. There are wars everywhere.

"If God has everything under control, do you mean God is running those wars?'"

Even an unregenerate columnist knew that wasn't right.

God is not ruling in this world. He is not ruling on the earth.

Thank God, He will one day!

But right now His will is not being carried out on the earth, except in the lives of those who surrender to Him.

That is easy to see if you will accept what the Bible says. The Bible says that God is not willing that any should perish, but that all should come to repentance (2 Peter 3:9). It is obvious that His will is not being carried out.

When individuals accept the Lord Jesus Christ as their Savior, it is carried out in their lives. But if God were running things and pushing His will off on people, since He is not willing that any should perish, He would make everybody get saved today and we would go into the Millennium tomorrow.

As I examined God's Word for the "why" behind John Wesley's statement, I saw a truth I had never seen before, though I had been in the ministry many years.

As I asked the Lord about it, He said to me, "Go back to the Book of Beginnings."

I knew He meant the Book of Genesis. I reread it. I had read it many times. I had heard it as a Sunday School boy. But I saw it in a different light this time.

I saw that God made the world and the fullness thereof. He made His man, Adam.

Then He said, "Adam, I give you dominion over all the work of my hands" (Gen. 1:26,27; Ps. 8:6).

God did not say, "I am going to dominate through you."

He said, "I give you dominion over all the work of my hands." Therefore Adam had dominion upon this earth and in this world. He was originally, in a sense, god of this world.

But Satan came and lied to Adam. Adam committed high treason and sold out to Satan. Then Satan became the god of this world.

Second Corinthians 4:4 calls Satan "the god of this world." As such, he has dominion. Where? In this world.

He will have that dominion, he will be god of this world, until Adam's lease runs out.

God cannot legally and justly move in and take away that dominion from the devil. The devil has dominion here. He has a right. He has Adam's lease. And God cannot do anything unless somebody down here asks Him.

Chapter 2

The Prayer of Intercession: One Kind of Prayer

> *Praying always with all prayer and supplication in the Spirit, and watching thereunto with all perseverance and supplication for all saints.*
>
> —Ephesians 6:18

Notice that says, *"Praying with ALL prayer . . . ."*

The *Amplified* translation reads, *"Pray . . . with ALL MANNER of prayer . . . ."*

Another translation reads, *"Praying with ALL KINDS of prayer . . . ."*

But the translation that really strikes a note in my own spirit is Goodspeed's. It reads, *"Use EVERY KIND of prayer and entreaty, and at every opportunity pray in the Spirit."* The Bible teaches several kinds of prayer—and the different rules governing them.

The church world makes a mistake in not differentiating between those different kinds of praying. We simply put all prayer in the same sack and shake it all out together. Many prayers are not working because people are using the wrong rules and laws.

In the field of sports, for instance, we have baseball, basketball, football, golf, tennis, etc. These are all kinds of sports—but they are not all played by the same rules.

Wouldn't it be confusing to play a baseball game with football rules, or vice versa?

The reason people are confused and have a prayer problem is that they have their rules and laws all mixed up together. They take rules which govern one kind of praying and try to apply them to other kinds of praying.

Speaking illustratively, they've got football, baseball, basketball, golf, and tennis rules supposedly all working together. They are confused. And so is their prayer life.

One common misconception people have is they think they should conclude every prayer with the words, "If it be thy will." They claim that is how Jesus prayed. However, Jesus prayed this way on only one occasion. That was in the Garden of Gethsemane when He prayed *the prayer of consecration*.

When they attempt to pray *the prayer of faith* (the prayer of petition, the prayer to change things), they conclude it with "if it be thy will." And their prayer is hindered because they are uncertain of His will—His Word.

They may say, "I don't understand why that didn't work." That would be like saying at a football game, "I don't see why someone doesn't hit a home run."

Don't be confused. Go to the Rulebook! Go to the Bible and see how to pray.

I will list here several kinds of prayers the Bible teaches. However, I cannot go into detail on them in this book. (I do have books on prayer which deal with them.)

★*The Prayer of Faith:* the prayer of petition, the prayer to change things (Matt. 21:22; Mark 11:24). This prayer, always to be based on God's revealed will in His Word, never contains an "if."

★*The Prayer of Consecration:* the prayer of consecration and dedication of our lives for God's use; to go anywhere and do anything. In this prayer we pray, "If it be thy will" (Luke 22:42).

★*The Prayer of Commitment:* casting your cares upon

the Lord in prayer (1 Peter 5:7).

　　The Prayer of Worship (Acts 13:1-4; Luke 24:52,53).

　　The Prayer of Agreement (Matt. 18:18-20).

　　Prayer in the Spirit: praying in tongues (1 Cor. 14:14,15).

　　United Prayer (Acts 4:23-31).

　　Intercessory Prayer: a prayer for others; and our subject in this book.

　　An intercessor is one who takes the place of another, or pleads another's case.

Chapter 3

Man's Need for an Intercessor

For he is not a man, as I am, that I should answer him, and we should come together in judgment. Neither is there any days man betwixt us, that might lay his hand upon us both.
—Job 9:32,33

The marginal rendering in my King James reference Bible for the word translated "days man" is "umpire." There is another reference reading "one who argues." In other words, there is no one to argue our cases on both sides.

The following translation is enlightening:

JOB 9:32,33 *(The Amplified Bible)*
32 For [God] is not a mere man, as I am, that I should answer Him, that we should come together in court.
33 There is no umpire between us, who might lay his hand upon us both [would that there were]!

Job needed one who would be able to lay his hand on him and a hand on God. He needed one to stand between him and God and plead his case.
—Reidt

God saw that there was no intercessor.

ISAIAH 59:16
16 And he saw that there was no man, and wondered that there was no intercessor: therefore his arm brought salvation unto him; and his righteousness, it sustained him.

God saw there was no intercessor, so He supplied the need. He sent Jesus.

Chapter 4

Jesus, Our Intercessor

Jesus came to bridge the gap between God and sinful man. Man needed someone to stand in the gap so he could get back to God. Man needed an Intercessor. Jesus' sacrifice established Him as the only fully trustworthy Intercessor for mankind. He is the only Intercessor for the people of this planet.

—Reidt

1 TIMOTHY 2:5
5 For there is one God, and ONE MEDIATOR BETWEEN GOD AND MEN, the man Christ Jesus.

He entered Heaven to appear in the presence of God for us.

—Reidt

HEBREWS 9:24
24 For Christ is not entered into the holy places made with hands, which are the figures of the true; but into heaven itself, now to appear in the presence of God FOR US.

He is our Intercessor at the right hand of the Father.

—Reidt

ROMANS 8:34
34 Who is he that condemneth? It is Christ that died, yea rather, that is risen again, who is even at the right hand of God, WHO ALSO MAKETH INTERCESSION FOR US.

He saves to the uttermost. His divine power can never cease for one moment.

—Reidt

HEBREWS 7:25
**25 Wherefore he is able also to save them to the
uttermost that come unto God by him, SEEING HE
EVER LIVETH TO MAKE INTERCESSION FOR
THEM.**

There flows from Jesus to the Father an unceasing
stream of prayer and love for all people and for those that
have accepted Him as Savior and Lord.

Conversely there flows from the Father to Jesus the
answer for us. Therefore there flows from Jesus to every
member of His Body abundant grace for every timely need.

He abideth forever. Regardless of circumstances,
regardless of how dark things look, regardless of how we
feel, He abides in us forever if we continue in His goodness
(Rom. 11:22).

He is our High Priest forever at the right hand of the
Father.

— Reidt

HEBREWS 7:16,17
**16 Who is made, not after the law of a carnal
commandment, but after the power of an endless life.
17 For he testifieth, Thou art a priest for ever after the
order of Melchisedec.**

How long is Jesus Christ our High Priest? Forever!

HEBREWS 8:1
**1 Now of the things which we have spoken this is the
sum: We have such an high priest, who is set on the
right hand of the throne of the Majesty in the heavens.**

As our High Priest He exercises every function of His
office in endless Life-Power. This endless Life-Power never
ceases for one moment. Our faith and experience of that
intercession need never fail because its flow is endless.

—Reidt

1 JOHN 2:1
1 My little children, these things write I unto you, that ye sin not. And if any man sin, we have an advocate with the Father, Jesus Christ the righteous.

Included in the idea of intercession is the fact that Jesus is our Advocate. Advocate means "intercessor, consoler."
—Reidt

W. E. Vine's Expository Dictionary of New Testament Words says of the Greek word PARAKLETOS translated advocate in First John 2:1, "It was used in a court of justice to denote a legal assistant, counsel for the defence, an advocate; then, generally, one who pleads another's cause, an intercessor, advocate. In the widest sense, it signifies a succourer, comforter."

When a person (Christian) sins, Jesus intercedes, and then consoles in the fact that the sin is forgiven and that the sin and its stain is washed away by His blood leaving the person pure and clean. However, it is the will of God that a person stop sinning (1 John 2:1; 5:3).
—Reidt

First John 2:1 is not written to encourage us to sin. God wants us to stop sinning. But thank God, He did not stop with saying, *"My little children, these things write I unto you, that ye sin not."* If He had, then when we failed, we'd think, *We're out now; that's the end of it.*

No, that's just half that verse. He goes on to say, *"And if any man sin, we have an advocate with the Father, Jesus Christ the righteous."*

We have an Intercessor! We have a Consoler!

1 JOHN 5:3
3 For this is the love of God, that we keep his

commandments: and his commandments are not grievous.

The love law of the family of God is, *"A new commandment I give unto you, That ye love one another; as I have loved you, that ye also love one another"* (John 13:34).

Every step outside of love is sin.

We tend to get our minds on dos and don'ts, but many Christians who abide perfectly by dos and don'ts are still sinning. How? By not walking in love.

Their attitudes are wrong. You need to maintain a love attitude toward your fellow man. If you do not, you are sinning.

Thank God for His Intercessor. Thank God for His standing in that place today to minister for us.

> Jesus spent about 3½ years in teaching and training His apostles. Since His ascension He has been interceding for about 2000 years for the people of this earth. What a dignity this adds to prayer.
>
> —Reidt

Jesus has been interceding 2000 years *for the people of this earth*—not just for the Church!

Notice Hebrews 7:25 again, *"Wherefore he is able also to save them to the uttermost THAT COME UNTO GOD* [This is talking about people coming unto God.] *by him, seeing he ever liveth to make intercession for them."*

Chapter 5

The Holy Spirit: Our Helper in Intercession

The Holy Spirit intercedes for us.
The Holy Spirit also *helps* us to intercede.

> **ROMANS 8:26,27**
> **26 Likewise the Spirit also HELPETH our infirmities: for we know not what we should pray for as we ought: but the Spirit itself [Himself] maketh intercession for us with groanings which cannot be uttered.**
> **27 And he that searcheth the hearts knoweth what is the mind of the Spirit, because he maketh intercession for the saints according to the will of God.**

Dr. T. J. McCrossan, who was a noted professor of Greek, included this enlightening insight into the Greek word translated "helpeth" in his book *Bodily Healing and the Atonement* (now available from Kenneth Hagin's Faith Library):

> . . . note well the word here translated "helpeth" *(sunantilambanetai)*. This is the present tense, 3rd person singular of the deponent verb *sunantilambanomai,* and comes from *sun,* together with; *anti,* against; and *lambano,* I take hold of. This word, therefore, means "to take hold against together with."
> Thus, in Romans 8:26 we are told that the Holy Ghost takes hold against our sicknesses together with someone. With whom? Why, with ourselves . . . .
>
> — McCrossan

Dr. McCrossan was dealing with only one side of infirmity (feebleness of body; sickness), but we can clearly see that the Holy Spirit helps by taking hold together with us against our infirmities.

If I said from the platform, "Some of you men stay after the service and help us move this piano off the platform," I would mean that I wanted them to take hold, together with someone else, against the weight of the piano.

The Holy Spirit helps. He takes hold together with us against the infirmity. If we do not take hold together with against—He has nothing to do. We must take hold together with first—then the Holy Spirit will help us.

Someone once said to me, "Since I found out the Holy Spirit is doing my praying for me, I don't do too much praying anymore."

Romans 8:26 does not say that the Holy Spirit does our praying for us. He *helps* us. If the Holy Spirit did our praying for us, that would make Him responsible for our prayer life, and that's out of line with the Bible.

Read what Jesus said in the Four Gospels relative to the Holy Spirit. For instance, *"And I will pray the Father, and he shall give you another Comforter, that he may abide with you for ever; Even the Spirit of truth; whom the world cannot receive, because it seeth him not, neither knoweth him: but ye know him; for he dwelleth with you, and shall be in you. I will not leave you comfortless ... But the Comforter, which is the Holy Ghost, whom the Father will send in my name, he shall teach you all things, and bring all things to your remembrance, whatsoever I have said unto you"* (John 14:16-18,26).

The Greek word PARACLETE here translated "Comforter" literally means "one called along side to help."

The *Amplified* translation gives the sevenfold meaning of the word: Comforter, Counselor, Helper, Intercessor, Advocate, Strengthener, Standby.

The Holy Spirit is not sent to do the Christians' work for them; He is sent to help them do it.

Jesus told the disciples to tarry in Jerusalem until they were baptized with the Holy Ghost. He said, " . . . *ye shall receive power, after that the Holy Ghost is come upon you: and ye shall be witnesses unto me . . . .* " (Acts 1:8).

One meaning of the Greek word translated power here is "ability." Another way to say it is this, "After the Holy Spirit comes upon you, you shall receive ability . . . . " Ability to do what? To be witnesses.

Now the Holy Spirit is not going to do the witnessing— you are going to do the witnessing with His ability.

Likewise the Holy Spirit will not do your praying for you—but you are going to be able to pray with His ability. He will *help* you do it.

We're the ones who are responsible for our lives.

We're the ones who are responsible to spread the Gospel.

We're the ones who are responsible to pray. The Holy Spirit is our helper.

Chapter 6

The Holy Spirit: Groanings and Travail

One way the Holy Spirit helps us in intercessory prayer is in groanings—and also in praying in other tongues.

People often quote Romans 8:26 and 27 in reference to the Holy Spirit's part in intercession. Yet to quote these two verses alone does not give their full meaning. They are linked to the verses before them.

I will print the entire passage here with capital letters to show continuity:

ROMANS 8:22-27

22 For we know that the whole creation GROANETH AND TRAVAILETH IN PAIN [Hold that in your mind; all these verses speak of groanings.] **together until now.**

23 And not only they, BUT OURSELVES ALSO, which have the firstfruits of the Spirit, EVEN WE OURSELVES GROAN WITHIN OURSELVES, waiting for the adoption, to wit, the redemption of our body.

24 For we are saved by hope: but hope that is seen is not hope: for what a man seeth, why doth he yet hope for? [This is not speaking about the new birth. It is written to people already born again. It is talking about hoping for the fullness of redemption when we have a new body.]

25 But if we hope for that we see not, then do we with patience wait for it.

26 LIKEWISE [or in the same manner, the Spirit helps us by groanings] **THE SPIRIT ALSO HELPETH OUR INFIRMITIES: for we know not what we should pray for as we ought: but the Spirit itself** [Himself] **MAKETH INTERCESSION FOR US WITH**

19

GROANINGS WHICH CANNOT BE UTTERED.
27 And he that searcheth the hearts knoweth what is the mind of the Spirit, BECAUSE HE MAKETH INTERCESSION FOR THE SAINTS ACCORDING TO THE WILL OF GOD.

All the creation is groaning and travailing in pain. The ultimate consciousness of pain resides in God because of His perfect love. Through our fellowship with God we are brought into fellowship with the suffering creation. Our consciousness of the groaning of the creation is much more acute than when we were outside the Kingdom of God, because we are united to God through Jesus Christ (John 15:5).

The Holy Spirit interprets to us God's consciousness of suffering and makes intercession with groanings that cannot be uttered.

—Reidt

The late P. C. Nelson was a noted linguist. Some 30 years ago, a secular magazine called him the leading authority of the day on Greek and the second-ranked authority on Hebrew. He could read and write 32 languages.

Nelson said that the Greek in Romans 8:26 actually implies, "with groanings that cannot be uttered in articulate speech."

They are uttered—but not in articulate speech. Articulate speech is your regular speech. These groanings—I know both from the Bible and from experience—come from within you, out of your spirit, but to be effective they must escape your lips.

Again it is the Holy Spirit's helping you to pray. You just cannot express them in your own words.

The New English Bible translates it, "through our

inarticulate groans the Spirit Himself is pleading for us."

The *Phillips* translation calls them "agonizing long-ings which never find words."

> We may not know how or what to ask in prayer so that our prayer will correspond with our real needs. The Holy Spirit moves us with groanings which we cannot express in words and helps us direct our desires to the proper objects. Also to help us to be specific is a part of the groanings. These groanings, yearnings, are according to the will of God and express His care for us. Although we cannot understand the groanings (Greek, sigh), they are intelligible to God. He always responds.
>
> In adverse circumstances or conditions the Holy Spirit intercedes with groanings.
>
> —Reidt

I've noticed in my own life that sometimes I go along and don't have too much of this. There is no particular need for it at the moment. But then, in time of adverse circumstances or conditions, those groanings begin to well up inside me—that is the Holy Spirit's helping us to pray.

You yield yourself to the Spirit in prayer and He uses you in this manner.

Take note of the word "likewise" in Romans 8:26. It means "in the same manner."

In the same manner as what? In the same manner as what was said before.

In other words, just as the whole creation groaneth and travaileth in pain . . . even we ourselves groan within ourselves . . . (and) LIKEWISE the Spirit also helpeth our infirmities . . . making intercession for us with groanings which cannot be uttered.

Until everything does come into complete harmony with the will of God, as Wilford Reidt said:

There will always be the need for the Holy Spirit to intercede with groanings. We may know the will of God but only the Holy Spirit knows how to effectively present the need. There are circumstances in which we are not sure of how to pray. We need the groaning of the Holy Spirit in intercession.

—Reidt

We will discuss groanings and travail further later in this book—especially in connection with interceding for the lost and interceding concerning the consummation of God's plan and work in the earth.

Chapter 7

The Holy Spirit and Our Infirmities

Likewise the Spirit also helpeth our INFIRMITIES . . . .

—Romans 8:26

What does the word "infirmities" mean in this setting?

W. E. Vine's Expository Dictionary of New Testament Words defines the Greek word as meaning: want of strength, weakness, indicating inability to produce results.

Our infirmities would keep us from producing prayer results were it not for our divine Helper, the Spirit of God.

Ignorance

"*Ignorance* is an infirmity," Reidt points out. "We do not always *know*."

Paul interceded for the Colossians that they would *know*. (And in his prayer we find a clue as to how to intercede for fellow Christians.)

COLOSSIANS 1:9
9 For this cause we also, since the day we heard it, DO NOT CEASE TO PRAY for you, and to desire that ye MIGHT BE FILLED WITH THE KNOWLEDGE OF HIS WILL IN ALL WISDOM AND SPIRITUAL UNDERSTANDING.

The will of God and the Word of God are connected.

God has given us His written Word to reveal to us His

will. We are to renew our minds with His Word so that the first thing which comes to mind in a given situation is what God has to say on the subject.

> **ROMANS 12:2**
> **2 And be not conformed to this world: but be ye transformed by the renewing of your mind, that ye may prove what is that good, and acceptable, and perfect, will of God.**

God has given us His Word. The Holy Spirit takes that Word and brings it to our remembrance. Then we know the will of God if we know the Word of God.

> **JOHN 14:26**
> **26 But the Comforter, which is the Holy Ghost, whom the Father will send in my name, he shall teach you all things, and bring all things to your remembrance, whatsoever I have said unto you.**

Then, thanks be unto God, for things the Word does not cover, we have an unction from the Holy One.

> **1 JOHN 2:20**
> **20 But ye have an unction from the Holy One, and ye know all things.**

Dullness of Perception

Dullness of perception is an infirmity. Jesus referred to this in Luke 24:25 when He said, "O fools, and slow of heart to believe all that the prophets have spoken."

Paul interceded for the Ephesians because of this condition . . . .

—Reidt

EPHESIANS 1:16-18
16 [I] cease not to give thanks for you, making mention of you in my prayers.
17 That the God of our Lord Jesus Christ, the Father of glory, MAY GIVE UNTO YOU THE SPIRIT OF WISDOM and REVELATION in the KNOWLEDGE OF HIM:
18 The EYES OF YOUR UNDERSTANDING BEING ENLIGHTENED; THAT YE MAY KNOW what is the hope of his calling, and what the riches of the glory of his inheritance in the saints . . . .

(Again, as in his prayer for the Colossians, Paul's Spirit-anointed prayer shows us how we can pray for ourselves and for other believers to overcome dullness of perception concerning things of the Lord.)

Because of this "dullness of perception" the Spirit has to intercede with groanings.

As we learn to know the Word and the will of God, the Spirit will not need to intercede for us so much in groanings.

We need the Scriptures to be opened up to us as Jesus did to the two on the road to Emmaus and to the apostles (Luke 24:13-45).

—Reidt

LUKE 24:45
45 Then opened he their understanding, that they might understand the scriptures.

The Holy Spirit is given to teach us all things (John 14:26). He teaches us directly in our own spirits. But He also teaches us through teachers who know the Word of God. God put teachers in the Church (Eph. 4:11,12). Do not limit the amount of knowledge you can acquire from God.

ROMANS 15:14
14 And I myself also am persuaded of you, my brethren, that ye also are full of goodness, FILLED WITH ALL KNOWLEDGE, able also to admonish one another.

That's where God wants us to be!

Chapter 8

Interceding Against the Infirmity of Sickness

Another definition of the word translated "infirmity" in Romans 8:26 is "feebleness of body, frailty, sickness."

Intercession is often necessary against this infirmity.

When I teach on faith and healing in crusades and seminars, I can only cover one side of it. The meetings are not long enough to cover the entire picture. Therefore I have one purpose in mind—to move people to believe God now and receive from God now. Thank God, a certain percentage of them can and will.

We know—because we have the Bible and the Bible imparts unto us the knowledge of God—that healing is provided for everyone. We know it is the highest and the perfect will of God that every believer not be sick, but live out his full length of time here below until his body wears out and he falls asleep in Jesus.

We've got to present God's perfect will or people won't know about it. But we also know from the natural standpoint that for a number of reasons that does not happen with everybody—even all of God's children.

(If it does not, it doesn't mean the people were not saved. It does not mean they did not go to Heaven.)

We know from the Old Testament that God made a covenant with Israel. He said to them, *"And ye shall serve the Lord your God, and he shall bless thy bread, and thy water; and I will take sickness away from the midst of thee. There shall nothing cast their young, nor be barren, in thy land: the number of thy days I will fulfil"* (Ex. 23:25,26).

Wasn't that God's perfect will? Yes!

But notice, it was conditional.

What was the condition? That they walk in His statutes and keep His commandments.

As long as Israel kept the covenant there was no sickness among them. No babies or young people died.

But then sickness and disease invaded them and people began dying young. Why? Because they did not keep their covenant.

Even in the household of the king a young child was sick and the prophet foretold the child would die.

How did the prophet know that? By the Spirit of God.

It was not the perfect will of God that the child die, but through sin the covenant was broken. The Spirit of God said what would happen under the circumstances.

The same thing that happened with Israel happens with individuals today. We have to tell people what God's plan is and what God's covenant is and what belongs to them. Healing is ours. Healing is in the atonement. Yet not everyone is walking in their New Covenant rights.

Sometimes—if they are bona fide baby Christians—you can exercise your faith for them. You can carry them on your faith for a while.

Sometimes you can get them to agree with you. You can join your faith with theirs in the prayer of agreement (Matt. 18:19). It works.

But there are still those who do not know, and who do not understand, for whom intercession must be made.

A denominational minister who still pastored his church told me how his wife had been marvelously healed by the power of God after medical science had given up on her case. Her healing brought them into the charismatic movement.

"Then," he said, "we began to get our eyes open to the

baptism in the Holy Spirit." They were relatively new in the things of the Spirit when his wife had an experience in intercession for healing.

A young wife and mother of three who attended his church regularly had to have open heart surgery. She died on the operating table. After some time she was resuscitated, but she did not regain consciousness.

The doctors said she would never regain consciousness—and that this was just as well, for her mind would never be right; she had been without oxygen to her brain for too long.

This pastor told me, "We comforted the young husband and prayed with him all we could—but we were so new in this . . . . Yet the woman persisted in living.

"The third night I woke up and suddenly realized my wife wasn't in bed. After a little while I got up to look for her. I heard groanings from the living room. I thought, *She got up and fell and hurt herself.* I found her lying flat on the living room floor groaning."

He got down beside her and said, "Honey, what's the matter?"

She said, "I don't know. I don't understand it, but I just can't let her die. I just can't do it."

For three nights, every night, she lay on the floor and groaned and prayed out loud all night long.

The next day, suddenly, that young woman in the hospital came to herself. The doctors were amazed. Her mind was clear. She was perfectly all right. She was restored to her husband and children.

Even though this pastor's wife was new in this, she began to make intercession for the woman mainly because the Spirit of God gave it to her—not because she worked it up.

How dependent we are upon the Holy Spirit in our prayer life.

In dealing with the sick, I find that sometimes the Spirit of God gives me intercession.

And there are times I have tried to get Him to but He does not. You cannot make the Spirit of God do anything. Instead of using the Spirit, let the Spirit use you.

Thirty years ago I went to a man's bedside to pray for his healing. And I couldn't even say the word "heal." I'd say, "Oh, God," and then instead of saying the word *"heal,"* I'd say, *"bless* this man." I tried to make my tongue say "heal" and it would not. I couldn't control my tongue.

I said, "Lord, why can't I pray for this man's healing? He's not old enough to die. You promised us a minimum of 70 or 80 years."

(In Psalm 91, He actually said, "with long life will I satisfy you." If we are not satisfied at the end of 70 or 80 years, we can go on until we are satisfied.)

But the Lord said to me, "Yes, but he was born again 36 years ago. I've been waiting on him to put away sin for 36 years. (Think about the patience of God!) He's never lived right over two weeks at a time in 36 years. So I judged him and turned him over to Satan for the destruction of the flesh that his spirit may be saved in the day of the Lord Jesus."

(That's in the Bible. Read the fifth chapter of First Corinthians and the last part of the eleventh chapter.)

Then the Spirit said to me, "You can't pray for his healing, but you can do this. Tell him you are going to lay your hands on him to be filled with the Holy Spirit and his last days will be better than his first."

I told him what the Lord said. When I laid my hand on his forehead, instantly, he started speaking with tongues.

I left and went my way. When I came back over a month later, he was dead and buried. But they told me he sat up in bed and sang and talked in tongues three days and nights. Then he had a glorious homegoing.

That wasn't God's perfect will for him. But it certainly beat going to hell.

I went off down the highway in my car, crying and singing, "Grace, grace, God's grace. Grace that is greater than all of our sins."

Sometimes I have tried to make intercession for people, and it would seem like I ran up against a blank wall, or down a blind alley. I just didn't get anywhere because the Spirit of God didn't take hold with me.

Identification

Sometimes in making intercession for others against physical sickness it will seem in the spirit—literally, physically it is not so—but it will seem in the spirit that the same thing fastens itself upon your body. You see, you are taking the place of another.

Sometimes I hurt just like they hurt. If they are sick at their stomach, I get sick to my stomach. If they can't breathe, I gasp for breath. I am identifying with them.

Since 1949, with only one exception, every time I have made intercession for the sick and taken on their symptoms, they always received their healing. And that one exception, Jesus appeared on the scene and said, "I have come to heal him, but he won't let me."

Chapter 9

The Intercession of the Believer

I exhort therefore, that, first of all, suppli-
cations, prayers, intercessions, and giving of
thanks, be made for all men; For kings, and for
all that are in authority; that we may lead a quiet
and peaceable life in all godliness and honesty.
                                          —1 Timothy 2:1,2

The Spirit of God, through the Apostle Paul, exhorted believers to put something first—not second, nor third, but first.

First of all, supplications (petitions), prayers, intercessions, and giving of thanks (gratitude; grateful language to God as an act of worship), are to be made for all men; for kings (or presidents), and for all who are in authority.

On what grounds can we do this?

On what basis can we petition, pray, intercede, and give thanks for others?

We can legally do it because *we are one with the Great Intercessor.*

One With the Great Intercessor

We have already talked about Jesus as Intercessor—and now we see that because we are one with Him, we are one with the Great Intercessor.

1 CORINTHIANS 6:17
17 But he that is joined unto the Lord is one spirit.

EPHESIANS 5:30
30 For we are members of his body, of his flesh, and of his bones.

2 PETER 1:4
4 Whereby are given unto us exceeding great and precious promises: that by these ye might be partakers of the divine nature, having escaped the corruption that is in the world through lust.

1 CORINTHIANS 12:27
27 Now ye are the body of Christ, and members in particular.

Christ is the Head. We are the Body. The head and the body are one. We are one with Him in carrying out His work in the earth.

He is the Great Intercessor. Therefore we are one with Him in His intercessory ministry.

We are one with Him in His ministry of reconciliation.

2 CORINTHIANS 5:18-20
18 And all things are of God, who hath reconciled us to himself by Jesus Christ, and hath given to us the ministry of reconciliation;
19 To wit, that God was in Christ, reconciling the world unto himself, not imputing their trespasses unto them; and hath committed unto us the word of reconciliation.
20 Now then we are ambassadors for Christ, as though God did beseech you by us: we pray you in Christ's stead, be ye reconciled to God.

We are partakers of His sufferings. (More about this later.)

2 CORINTHIANS 1:7
7 And our hope of you is stedfast, knowing, that as ye

are partakers of the sufferings, so shall ye be also of the consolation.

Wilford Reidt capsules it like this: "He is our great Intercessor. He is the great Intercessor for all mankind. As members of His Body, the Church, we partake in that intercession."

Therefore, our intercession will find its pattern in Him.

Chapter 10

Ingredients for Successful Intercession

Love—the God-kind of love, "agape"—is the first prerequisite for successful intercession. And if you are a child of God, you have this kind of love.

ROMANS 5:5
5 ... the love [agape] of God is shed abroad in our hearts by the Holy Ghost which is given unto us.

When you were born again, God became your Father. He is a love God. You are a love child of a love God. You are born of God, and God is love, so you are born of love. The nature of God is in you. And the nature of God is love.

Ours is a love family. Everyone in the family has it, or else they are not in the family.

Now they may not be exercising it. They may be like the one-talent guy who wrapped his talent in a napkin and buried it. But the Bible declares that the love of God has been shed abroad in our hearts by the Holy Ghost. That means the God-kind of love has been shed abroad in our spirits.

This is a love family. Love is the basis for all the activity of the Body of Christ in the earth.

1 THESSALONIANS 4:9
9 But as touching brotherly love ye need not that I write unto you: for ye yourselves are taught of God to love one another.

The love law of the family of God is:

JOHN 13:34
**34 A new commandment I give unto you, That ye love
one another; as I have loved you, that ye also love one
another.**

We are also commanded to love our enemies:

MATTHEW 5:44,45
**44 But I say unto you, Love your enemies, bless them
that curse you, do good to them that hate you, and
pray for them which despitefully use you, and
persecute you;**
**45 That ye may be the children of your Father which is
in heaven: for he maketh his sun to rise on the evil and
on the good, and sendeth rain on the just and on the
unjust.**

The reason we can do this—love our enemies, bless
them that curse us, do good to them that hate us, and pray
for them which despitefully use us, and persecute us—is
because of the manner of love the Father has bestowed
upon us:

1 JOHN 3:1
**1 Behold, what manner of love the Father hath
bestowed upon us, that we should be called the sons of
God . . . .**

Your Will and Love

This *agape* love—this God-kind of love—involves the
choice of your will.

That love is inside your spirit if you are born again. But
you are the one who has to will to put it into practice. You
choose to let that love loose from within you.

We can choose to love all people—even our enemies.

Almost anyone can love those who love them, but the Bible tells us to love our enemies.

> We choose to love all people, even the unlovable. We love as God loves. It involves (the) giving of our lives for the benefit of mankind. This does not merely refer to dying physically. It mainly refers to our being willing to give up our own will and way and take time to pray and intercede for all men.
>
> —Reidt

God loved us while we were yet sinners and sent Christ to die for us. We are to love the same way. We give our lives for mankind.

This is where suffering comes in. This is how we enter into His suffering.

You're not suffering for Christ when you are sick with pneumonia, or flu, or measles, or cancer. That's not His suffering. He didn't have measles. He didn't have pneumonia or leprosy.

We enter into His sufferings for humanity.

It involves sacrifice. It involves giving our lives for the benefit of mankind.

There is suffering and sacrifice in giving up your own will and life to intercede for others.

Compassion

> Love is the basis for all Christian activity. Compassion is an ingredient of divine love.
>
> —Reidt

How do we know this is so?

Because God so loved the world that He gave Jesus. And Jesus so loved us that He gave Himself for us. And in

His earthly ministry, again and again we see compassion.

As we look at that wonderful truth, remember that Jesus said, *"He that hath seen me hath seen the Father"* (John 14:9). If you want to see God, look at Jesus. Jesus is the will of God in action. Jesus is the love of God in action. And in His earthly ministry, He was moved with compassion . . . .

> **MATTHEW 9:36-38**
> 36 But when he saw the multitudes, he was moved with compassion on them, because they fainted, and were scattered abroad, as sheep having no shepherd.
> 37 Then saith he unto his disciples, The harvest truly is plenteous, but the labourers are few.
> 38 Pray ye therefore the Lord of the harvest, that he will send forth labourers into his harvest.

> Jesus had compassion on the people and asked us to share in that compassion by praying that the Lord of the Harvest would send laborers into the field.
>
> —Reidt

Jesus was moved with compassion and healed the sick:

> **MATTHEW 14:14**
> 14 And Jesus went forth, and saw a great multitude, and was moved with compassion toward them, and he healed their sick.

Jesus' compassion led to the feeding of the four thousand:

> **MATTHEW 15:32**
> 32 Then Jesus called his disciples unto him, and said, I have compassion on the multitude, because they continue with me now three days, and have nothing to

eat: and I will not send them away fasting, lest they faint in the way.

In His compassion, Jesus healed the blind:

MATTHEW 20:34
34 So Jesus had compassion on them, and touched their eyes: and immediately their eyes received sight, and they followed him.

Compassion led to the healing of the leper:

MARK 1:40,41
40 And there came a leper to him, beseeching him, and kneeling down to him, and saying unto him, If thou wilt, thou canst make me clean.
41 And Jesus, moved with compassion, put forth his hand, and touched him, and saith unto him, I will; be thou clean.

In His compassion, Jesus healed every person who asked (Mark 6:56, Luke 6:19, Matt. 4:23,24).

Jesus taught His disciples to share in His compassion by sending out the twelve (Luke 9:1-6) and the seventy (Luke 10:1-19).

His compassion was to be carried on after His Ascension as He made healing one of the signs of the believer (Mark 16:16-18).

His compassion was demonstrated after His Ascension (Acts 5:15,16; 19:11,12; 28:8,9).

In every instance where Jesus was moved with compassion, the person or persons were delivered.

Human sympathy says, "I know how you feel; I'm so sorry."

Divine compassion says, "I feel how you feel." And it brings deliverance.

Jesus felt as Mary and Martha felt as He groaned within and also wept.

—Reidt

JOHN 11:33,35
33 When Jesus therefore saw her weeping, and the
Jews also weeping which came with her, he groaned
in the spirit, and was troubled . . .
35 Jesus wept.

Jesus' compassion brought deliverance. If we have the divine compassion of Jesus, there will be deliverance. But I think too much of the time we've tried to bring deliverance without the divine compassion. That's where prayer and intercession come in.

Weeping with them that weep brings deliverance (Rom. 12:15).

Dr. John G. Lake is known for his ministry well marked with apostolic ideals. He did an amazing work in South Africa just after the turn of the century.

So many healings took place in his tabernacle in Johannesburg, report of them reached the leaders of the nation. Some of the top government people sought him for help on the behalf of the wife of a government official.

When Lake went to her home, he found her bedridden with terminal cancer. He determined that she was a Christian. Then he began to give her Scripture to teach her about divine healing and to get her faith activated.

She made a decision to trust God for her healing. The doctors had given her up to die and were only giving her pain relievers to keep her comfortable. But she decided to stop all drugs.

She said, "If I'm going to trust God for my healing, and I am, then I'm going to throw myself completely over on His mercy."

"She was in such pain," Lake said, "that one of the ministers of the church and I stayed at her bedside around the clock, praying. As we prayed, she would get relief."

One morning, after having prayed all night, Lake went home just long enough to bathe and shave. Then he started back.

"When I came within two blocks of the house," Lake said, "I heard her screaming in pain. At the sound of those screams, somehow I seemed to enter into a divine compassion . . . ."

That's what you do in intercession.

Lake entered into the sufferings of Jesus. He began to feel just like Jesus feels. For Jesus can be touched with the feelings of our infirmities (Heb. 4:15).

Lake said, "I found myself running those last two blocks without even thinking what I was doing. Without thinking, I rushed into the room, sat down on the edge of the bed, picked up that emaciated body in my arms like a baby, and began to weep. While I was weeping, she was perfectly healed."

Somehow, the compassion of Jesus, the love of God, was able to permeate his heart, his spirit.

Dedicated believers can enter into that area of compassion by one way—and you will not get there any other way—fellowship with God.

You cannot fellowship with God . . . you cannot sit in the Presence of the Great God of this universe . . . without His love permeating your being . . . without His compassion flowing into you.

And it is when you can get into this place that you will be able to do as Jesus said . . .

JOHN 14:12
12 Verily, verily, I say unto you, He that believeth on me, the works that I do shall he do also; and greater works than these shall he do; because I go unto my Father.

The works that He did were born out of love and
compassion. The works that the believing ones shall do are
products of sharing in His ministry of love and compassion.

Chapter 11

Knowing God's Love

And to know the love of Christ, which passeth knowledge, that ye might be filled with all the fulness of God.

—Ephesians 3:19

To intercede effectively, you must know the great love God has for all humanity.

> He sends the rain on the just and the unjust (Matt. 5:45).
> He makes the sun to rise on the evil and the good (Matt. 5:45).
> He is kind to the unthankful and to the evil (Luke 6:35).
> —Reidt

Since the love of God is in us, and the love of God has been shed abroad in our hearts, we are to be kind like God is kind—to the unthankful and to the evil.

Whosoever Will

> Jesus purchased a gift of salvation for anyone who would accept it (Eph. 2:8; Rev. 22:17). God commands all men everywhere to repent (Acts 17:30). His hand of mercy is extended to all mankind.
>
> Our intercession for all men is not so much for God to extend His mercy. This He has already done through Jesus.
>
> *Our intercession is mainly to break the bondage that the devil has over men.*
>
> The devil has blinded men (2 Cor. 4:3,4). We are to loose the sinner from the blindness that he may see the Light.
>
> Fasting, prayer, and intercession are among the weapons of our warfare that pull down the strongholds of the enemy (2 Cor. 10:4).
> —Reidt

One afternoon a number of years ago, I was lying across my bed resting between the morning and evening service. I had my Bible and another book and I was studying. Into my spirit—not into my mind—came an understanding of some of these things I'd never had before. I saw this Scripture in a way I'd never seen it to that time:

> 2 CORINTHIANS 4:3,4
> 3 But if our gospel be hid, it is hid to them that are lost:
> 4 In whom the god of this world hath blinded the minds of them which believe not, lest the light of the glorious gospel of Christ, who is the image of God, should shine unto them.

I saw how we had missed it in praying for the lost.

I don't mean it unkindly, but just to say, "God save Uncle John and Aunt Lucy," does about as much good as it does to twiddle your thumbs and say, "Twinkle, twinkle, little star." God has already done all He's going to do about saving them.

But I didn't know that. Until that afternoon. I'd been praying like that about my own relatives.

That afternoon, I heard the Lord say to my spirit, "No human in his right mind would drive his car down the highway 100 miles an hour, past blinking red warning lights, past signs that said, 'Danger! Bridge out!' and plunge himself out into eternity. But a drunk man would—a doped man would. The same thing is true spiritually. No man in his right mind would plunge himself out into eternity without God. But the god of this world has blinded their minds."

He gave me this Scripture, *"In whom the god of this world hath blinded the minds . . . ."* (2 Cor. 4:4).

I could hear the Spirit of God challenging me, "You've approached it wrongly. You've worked on the wrong end of the thing. You fasted and prayed that I would do something and I've done all I'm ever going to do. The blood has already been shed. The Gospel has already been given. The light is already here. It can't shine in because of what the devil has done. What you've got to do is break that power over them."

Intercession does not change God—God never changes.

Prayer does not change God. Prayer changes you and it changes others. It does not change God.

I saw what I had to do for my brother, Dub. I'd been fasting and praying that God would save him off and on for 15 years, and if it ever did any good, I couldn't tell it. Dub was the black sheep of the family. Anything you could mention, he'd done. I knew if it would work on him, it would work on anyone.

I rose up off the bed with my Bible in one hand, and the other hand lifted, saying, "In the Name of the Lord Jesus Christ, I break the power of the devil over my brother Dub's life, and I claim his deliverance. (That meant I claimed his deliverance from that blindness, that bondage of Satan.) And I claim his full salvation in the Name of the Lord Jesus Christ."

Within three weeks, my brother was born again.

Here is where intercession comes in—we are to loose the sinner from the blindness that he may see the light.

If we can get people to see God as He really is, they'll want to love Him.

We are one with the great Intercessor in His ministry of reconciliation.

Let's look at this Scripture again in the *Amplified* translation:

2 CORINTHIANS 5:19 *(Amplified)*
19 It was God (personally present) in Christ, reconciling and restoring the world to favor with Himself, not counting up and holding against [men] their trespasses [but cancelling them]; and committing to us the message of reconciliation—of the restoration to favor.

Whom did He reconcile unto Himself? The world!

Whose trespasses are canceled? The world's!

That's what will be so terrible—people will go to hell, and when they get there, they'll find out we hadn't told them the truth. We hadn't told them everything was canceled out.

That's how God is kind to the unthankful and the evil. And He has given to us that message, that word of reconciliation.

Yet we have preached, "God is going to get you if you don't watch out. He's after you."

People have trained their children, saying, "Don't do that. Jesus won't love you if you do that."

That's a lie. He may not want them to do it, but He'll still love them anyhow.

Telling children, "God won't love you, if you do that," causes them to grow up with their minds blinded to the light of His love. And it's very difficult to get that kind of teaching out of people.

He has given to us the ministry of reconciliation.

We used to think we had to preach people under conviction. So we went out and beat them over the head, so to speak.

No! The Spirit of God will convict them.

Ours is the ministry of reconciliation. When we can get people to see God as He really is, they will want to love Him.

Chapter 12

Identification

We must identify with the one for whom we are interceding.

Jesus identified with Mary and Martha in the death of Lazarus. They were groaning and weeping. He groaned within and wept. He went to the grave and raised Lazarus from the dead.

Romans 12:15 brings in focus the idea of identification with others. *"Rejoice with them that do rejoice, and weep with them that weep."* The real believer can go from the house of rejoicing . . . to the house of weeping and weep with them.

Paul identified with the Jews that he might gain the Jews. Paul identified to them without law as without law (being not without law to God, but under law to Christ) that he might gain them that are without law. To the weak he became as weak that he might gain the weak. He said that he was made all things to all men, that he by all means might save some (1 Cor. 9:19-22).

—Reidt

The identification we are speaking of is that identification with the object that brings deliverance.

Jesus Christ, the great Intercessor, is our example. He identified with man when He, who had always existed in the form of God, emptied Himself and took the form of a bond servant, *" . . . and was made in the likeness of men: and being found in fashion as a man, he humbled himself, and became obedient unto death, even the death of the cross"* (Phil. 2:7,8).

Jesus Christ identified with fallen man to bring our deliverance.

As one with Him, we identify with the lost in intercession.

Chapter 13

Interceding for the Lost

> *Who hath heard such a thing? who hath seen such things? Shall the earth be made to bring forth in one day? or shall a nation be born at once? for as soon as Zion travailed, she brought forth her children.*
>
> —Isaiah 66:8

Many have looked at this verse and thought it referred only to the rebirth of Israel as a nation. Yet most Old Testament prophecy has a twofold application—first the natural, then the spiritual. Isaiah is prophesying that Israel will be reborn as a nation in the natural, and that in the spiritual, Zion will travail and bring forth her children.

Who is Zion?

The New Testament tells us that the New Covenant believer is not come to Mount Sinai where Moses received the Ten Commandments under the Old Covenant—but that we are come to Mount Zion. It calls the Church, Mount Zion.

HEBREWS 12:18-23
18 For ye are not come unto the mount that might be touched, and that burned with fire, nor unto blackness, and darkness, and tempest,
19 And the sound of a trumpet, and the voice of words; which voice they that heard intreated that the word should not be spoken to them any more:
20 (For they could not endure that which was commanded, And if so much as a beast touch the mountain, it shall be stoned, or thrust through with a dart:

21 And so terrible was the sight, that Moses said, I
exceedingly fear and quake:)
22 BUT YE ARE COME UNTO MOUNT SION, and
unto the city of the living God, the heavenly
Jerusalem, and to an innumerable company of angels,
23 TO THE GENERAL ASSEMBLY AND CHURCH
OF THE FIRSTBORN, which are written in heaven,
and to God the Judge of all, and to the spirits of just
men made perfect,
24 And to Jesus the mediator of the new covenant, and
to the blood of sprinkling, that speaketh better things
than that of Abel.

Notice this calls the Church of the general assembly of
the firstborn, "Mount Zion." And our text in Isaiah 66:8
said that, *"as soon as Zion travailed, she brought forth her
children."*

GALATIANS 4:19
19 My little children, of whom I travail in birth again
until Christ be formed in you.

Paul is writing to the churches throughout Galatia
(Gal. 1:2). He intimates that he travailed in birth for them
to be saved in the beginning. (Now he is travailing
"again.")

We talk about making conversions. God does not
mention conversions—He wants births. *You must be born
again!*

You cannot have births without having travail. The
picture here is of a woman having a baby.

(Now I do not mean that one must come to the altar and
travail to be born again. The baby does not birth itself. But
for true births out of the kingdom of darkness and into the
kingdom of light, some intercessor, somewhere, has
travailed.)

> Paul travailed. It was a spiritual activity. It is an
> intense suffering in the inner man. It is comparable to the
> pangs of natural childbirth. It involves real intercession. I
> had a friend, now with the Lord, who travailed in prayer
> and intercession until you would think his heart would
> break literally. Sure it is hard on the outer man.
>
> —Reidt

I've been there myself, again and again. I could give any number of illustrations. This is one of the most outstanding, however.

It happened the first Friday night of December 1953 in Phoenix, Arizona, where I was conducting a meeting.

During the meeting I stayed in the home of one of the families in the church. After the Friday night service they invited their three married daughters and their husbands to come to the home for refreshments and a time of visiting.

We men were seated in the living room talking. The women were in the kitchen preparing to serve the food.

Suddenly, I had an urge to pray. Now, don't misunderstand me; nobody made me do it, but there was a burden about it. An urge to pray just seemed to fall upon me.

I knew these folks would understand such a thing. (If they would not have, I would have excused myself and gone to the privacy of my bedroom to pray.) So I said to our host, "I've got to pray, and I have to pray now."

Brother F. called the ladies from kitchen, "Just forget about the food. Brother Hagin's got a burden to pray. Let's all just join him."

I knelt beside a large chair in the living room. The moment my knees touched the floor I was in the spirit. I lifted my voice, praying in other tongues and groanings.

It seemed like down deep within me I was hurting so badly I was about to deliver a baby. In travail there's pain—there are groanings.

I knew I was interceding. An intercessor is one who takes the place of another. When that spirit of intercession for the lost is upon you, you'll feel within your own being that you are lost. You know you are not. You know you are a child of God. But you take upon yourself the condition the other person is in. That person is lost. So you feel lost.

I've had people come to me many times saying something like this, "Brother Hagin, I know I'm saved and filled with the Holy Spirit, but sometimes in the service when God begins to move, I start to feel on the inside just like I'm lost myself. When the altar call is given, I wonder if I should go to the altar myself. I wonder if perhaps I'm not right with God."

"That's intercession," I explain to them. "That's the Spirit of God trying to roll the burden of some lost soul off on someone. He was searching through the congregation to find someone He could use.

"When that happens again, if you can't contain yourself, and the service is still going on, get up and go to a place of prayer. Otherwise, sit there quietly and groan within yourself, until the person you are interceding for responds to the call of God."

There is something out here in this area that we need to learn again. The art of intercession is a lost art among us. We'll never really have the depth of the move of the Spirit of God until we have that kind of intercession.

I prayed that Friday night in Phoenix with groanings, and tears, and other tongues for about an hour. I knew I was interceding for someone who was lost. And I knew to keep at it until I had a note of victory.

(A note of victory—that is when the burden lifts, and you feel light, wonderful, and blessed. Or, when you begin to sing in other tongues. Or, when you begin to laugh instead of groan. In other words, you have whatever it is you are praying about.)

Once in a great while, the Lord will let me know what or whom I am praying about. That Friday night, He let me know. He gave me a vision.

I saw the church where I was holding the meeting full of people.

I saw myself at the pulpit preaching.

I heard myself preach a sermon I'd never preached before. I heard myself give four points to this sermon. (I got a brand new sermon which I preached the following Sunday night.)

I saw myself finish the sermon, then lean over the pulpit and point to a man sitting the second seat from the front.

I heard myself say as I pointed to him, "Friend, God shows me you are past 70 years and that you've been brought up to believe that there is no hell. But He told me to tell you that you have one foot in hell right now, and the other one is slipping in."

I saw that man leave the pew, come and kneel in the altar, and be saved.

I knew I was making intercession for him. I knew I was travailing in prayer for him.

The folks present knew I'd seen something. So they asked me. I told them. I described the man to them. I described how he was dressed.

The following Sunday night everything came to pass exactly as I had seen it on the preceding Friday.

Those people who had prayed with me told me after the

service, "Brother Hagin, we had that fellow located before you ever got to the service. He was sitting where you said he'd be sitting. He was dressed just the way you saw him. We'd never seen him before." Nobody in that church had ever seen him. So they wouldn't have known to pray. But the Holy Spirit knew.

The man was saved along with others. After the service he came to hug the pastor and me.

He said to the pastor, "This preacher here said I was past 70. I'm 72. This is the first time I've ever been inside a church building. The preacher said I was raised to believe there is no hell. My parents were Universalists. They taught me that there is no hell.

"This preacher told me that God told him to tell me I had one foot in hell and the other was slipping. I know exactly what He meant. That's one reason why I came to Phoenix. I'm from up north where it's cold. But I had a severe heart attack and my doctor thought it would help my health to come here."

Somebody said, "He got saved Sunday night." But it really happened on Friday night when I was travailing in birth.

Do you know why babies are not being born into churches today? (Oh, some have a lot of conversions, but few births.) It is because there is no travail—no groanings.

And when some people begin to travail and groan in prayer, others are ready to throw them out.

Years ago, I ministered in a Full Gospel church that was running several hundreds in the Sunday morning services. And on Sunday night the building was almost full.

They had a dear old lady, dear old Grandma Greer, who was at that time 80 some odd years of age. She'd been in

Pentecost since the turn of the century. Away back around 1906 she had been baptized in the Holy Spirit. She knew something about travailing and waiting on God. (The old-timers did.) She would pray at the altar, groaning and praying in other tongues in the spirit of travail—carrying the entire thing, probably, on her own back.

Three years later I came back to this same church. Instead of having the building full for Sunday morning services, they had about 80 or 90 people. On Sunday night they had 35 to 50.

"What happened?" I asked someone.

One of the members said, "Do you remember old Grandma Greer?"

"Yes."

"Well, she was in the altar praying like she always did, and the new pastor got up and said, 'We're not going to have any of that around here.' "

He put a stop to it. They had no more babies being born, because there was no travailing. When Zion travails she brings forth her children.

Chapter 14

Until Christ Be Formed in You

My little children, of whom I travail in birth
again until Christ be formed in you.
                                    —Galatians 4:19

Paul had travailed—groaned and prayed in other tongues—for these people and they were born again. (Travail carries the idea of a woman travailing in birth with pain and agony and groanings.)

Now Paul says he is travailing *again* until Christ be formed in you.

He travailed for them as sinners to be birthed into the kingdom of God—now he is travailing for them as Christians that they might become mature, that they might grow up and not be baby Christians.

There is a similarity between spiritual growth and physical growth. No one is born a full-grown human. In the natural, people are born babies and they grow up. No one is born a full-grown Christian. They are born babies. Then they are to grow up, spiritually.

The Bible says, *"As newborn babes, desire the sincere milk of the word, that ye may grow thereby"* (1 Peter 2:2).

These churches of Galatia were trying to get back under the law instead of walking on in grace. Paul was alarmed. So he was interceding, praying, travailing for them that they mature and grow.

Epaphras did the same thing for the Colossian Christians and those in Laodicea and Hierapolis.

COLOSSIANS 4:12,13
12 Epaphras, who is one of you, a servant of Christ,

> saluteth you, always labouring fervently for you in
> prayers, that ye may stand perfect [mature] and
> complete in all the will of God.
> 13 For I bear him record, that he hath a great zeal for
> you and them that are in Laodicea, and them in
> Hierapolis.

*W. E. Vine's Expository Dictionary of New Testament
Words* gives this meaning for the Greek word PANOS
which is translated "labouring" in verse 12: denotes
labours, toil; the consequence of toil, viz., distress,
suffering, pain. (This word is translated pain in
Revelation 16:10,11; 21:4.)

Vine also says that the word translated "zeal" in verse
13 is this same word PANOS in the best manuscripts.

The *Centenary Translation of the New Testament*
translates verse 12 like this: *"Epaphras, one of yourselves,
salutes you, a slave of Christ who is always agonizing for
you in his prayers, that you may stand firm, mature, and
fully assured in all the will of God."*

I remember particularly the wonderful experience
with God a young woman had when she came to the altar
during a revival meeting I was holding. She was
gloriously saved and gloriously baptized in the Holy
Spirit. Oh! what a glow was upon her face.

Just a little less than a year later, I was back in the
area and I inquired about her because of the very unusual
and marvelous experience she'd had with God.

"Oh," they said, with their faces dark and frowning,
"she's backslidden."

I said, "Oh, I hate that."

They said, "Yes, we do, too."

Then, just as plainly, the Spirit of God spoke up on the
inside of me and said, "Yes, and the church is to blame for

it. The church is responsible for it."

I couldn't understand that for the longest time. How could the church be responsible for somebody's backsliding?

Then I saw it in Galatians 4:19. *"My little children, of whom I travail in birth again until Christ be formed in you."*

You see, that church just saw her get saved and baptized in the Holy Spirit. Then they said, "Well, she's got it made now."

But she was a baby. They should have continued to intercede and hold her up in prayer. Because they did not, when judgment day comes, God will hold that church responsible. He is going to require of every church reponsibility for the babies born at its altars.

"What did you do with them?" will be the question. "Did you teach them? Did you continue to pray for them? Or, if they made a mistake, did you knock them down and say, 'You backslidden buzzard, get right with God or get out of here: one of the two' "?

While people are babies spiritually, somebody has to carry them. Somebody has to feed them. Somebody has to care for them.

This is one place where the ministry of intercession comes in. Somebody has to intercede—to take the place of another.

Intercessors need to hold them up as they're learning to walk.

When my children or grandchildren fell as they were learning to walk, I didn't slap them. I got hold of them and loved them and said, "Just keep at it, honey. You'll learn."

In many cases, in praying for Christians, such travail is not necessary because they are not so tightly bound as the Galatian church seemed to be.

Learn to listen to the Spirit of God and pray as He directs.

Chapter 15

What Is "Praying in the Spirit"?

Intercessory prayer can be made two ways.

(1) With your understanding. (In your own language.)

(2) In the spirit. (In other tongues.)

Since praying in the spirit is so important, I am including this chapter, which covers a broader scope than intercession.

What is praying in the spirit?

EPHESIANS 6:18
18 Praying always with all prayer and supplication IN THE SPIRIT, and watching thereunto with all perseverance and supplication for all saints.

What does that mean in this verse, *"Praying . . . in the Spirit . . . . "*?

I faced this question many years ago as a Baptist pastor. I somehow knew inside me that whatever it was, I wasn't doing it.

I wanted to know. I asked people.

Do you know what most people thought praying in the spirit was?

They thought it meant praying with just a little more vim, vigor, and vitality!

Then, too, Jude's statement written to believers puzzled me.

JUDE 20
20 But ye, beloved, building up yourselves on your most holy faith, PRAYING IN THE HOLY GHOST.

I asked myself, "What is praying in the Holy Ghost?"
Whatever it was, I felt I wasn't doing it.

Now my head told me I was "praying in the spirit" and "praying in the Holy Ghost."

But my heart told me, "You are not."

So I set out to find out for sure what those expressions mean.

I thought, *Paul is doing the writing here in Ephesians where he speaks of "praying in the spirit." Did he ever say anything anywhere else about praying in the spirit? If he did, then he is talking about the same thing, wherever he speaks of it.*

So I began to run references on this phrase in Paul's writings. They led me to the 14th chapter of First Corinthians.

Now I hadn't gotten into the 14th chapter of First Corinthians too much. The first Sunday of each quarter, I preached from the 11th chapter just before we took the Lord's Supper. I would skip the 12th chapter and preach about love in the 13th chapter. Then I would skip over the 14th chapter and preach about the Resurrection in the 15th chapter. I was almost afraid of the 12th and 14th chapters.

But I could see that if I was going to find out about praying in the spirit, I had to get there, because it is there that Paul said something about it. I found out that he said . . . .

> **1 CORINTHIANS 14:2**
> 2 For he that speaketh in a unknown tongue speaketh not unto men, but unto God: for no man understandeth him; howbeit IN THE SPIRIT he speaketh mysteries.

In the spirit! In the spirit! In the spirit he speaketh mysteries! There it was!

Well, if speaking with tongues was praying in the spirit in the 14th chapter of First Corinthians, then when Paul wrote of praying in the spirit in Ephesians 6:18, he meant the same thing!

Now notice something:

> 1 CORINTHIANS 14:14,15
> 14 For if I pray in an unknown tongue, my spirit prayeth, but my understanding is unfruitful.
> 15 What is it then? I will pray with the spirit, and I will pray with the understanding also: I will sing with the spirit, and I will sing with the understanding also.

Let's read those same two verses from the *Amplified Bible*:

> 1 CORINTHIANS 14:14,15 *(Amplified)*
> 14 For if I pray in an [unknown] tongue, my spirit [by the Holy Spirit within me] prays, but my mind is unproductive—bears no fruit and helps nobody.
> 15 Then what am I to do? I will pray with my spirit—by the Holy Spirit that is within me; but I will also pray intelligently—with my mind and understanding; I will sing with my spirit—by the Holy Spirit that is within me; but I will sing (intelligently) with my mind and understanding also.

Paul said, "*I* will pray with my spirit . . . *I* will pray with my understanding." He said *he* would do it.

If praying in tongues is not for us today, then there is no way we can pray in the spirit today.

And yet, we are spirit beings. We need to pray out of our spirits and not just out of our heads.

Paul is talking here about two kinds of praying: (1)

mental praying, and (2) spiritual praying.

Mental praying is "with the understanding," with the mind. The church world as a whole has tried too long to get by on only one kind of praying—mental praying.

Yet we cannot succeed with just mental praying alone. Why not? God's Word gives the answer in Romans 8:26. There are times when we do not know how to pray. It would be impossible in these situations for mental praying alone to get the job done. Spiritual praying is required.

Spiritual praying is praying out of your spirit in utterances, in a tongue that is unknown to you, and sometimes in groaning—all of which escape your lips.

> **ROMANS 8:26**
> 26 Likewise the Spirit also helpeth our infirmities: for we know not what we should pray for as we ought: but the Spirit itself [Himself] maketh intercession for us with groanings which cannot be uttered.

We may not always understand the entire situation surrounding a matter about which we are praying. But the Holy Spirit does. When we allow Him to pray through us, to help us in our prayer life, we will see amazing answers to our prayers.

Every Spirit-filled believer can expect the Holy Spirit to help him in making intercession in the spirit, in other tongues. And that is our subject. But I want to mention some other benefits and uses of praying in tongues.

Praying in the Spirit
Magnifying God

> **ACTS 10:46**
> 46 For they heard them speak with tongues, and magnify God . . . .

Praying in the spirit, with tongues, is a way in which we can magnify God.

For years, as a minister, I prayed—and had wonderful times in prayer. I used to go down to the barn and get up in the hay loft to pray—and I had marvelous times of prayer there.

But I went away from those times disappointed, though I was blessed. I would try to tell God how much I loved Him. I would use all the descriptive adjectives at my disposal to tell God how wonderful He is. I would exhaust my vocabulary and leave that place of prayer with my spirit feeling I had not said what I wanted to say.

My spirit felt cheated. Although my head did not realize it, my spirit wanted to pray, too—apart from the understanding.

Now, one of the things I appreciate most about being filled with the Holy Spirit is praying with tongues. From that day in 1937 when I was first Spirit-filled to this, I have worshiped and communicated with God, praying and singing in tongues, every single day. And I never have left that place of prayer feeling that I didn't say what I wanted to say, because my spirit was enabled by the Holy Spirit who indwells me to say what it wanted to say.

If you are not doing so already, I invite you to come on in and communicate with God supernaturally. God wants to do so much more for you. He wants to communicate with you in a better way. Know the joy of fellowshiping with the Lord in the spirit.

Praying in the Spirit
To Edify Yourself

JUDE 20
20 But ye, beloved, building up yourselves on your most holy faith, praying in the Holy Ghost.

1 CORINTHIANS 14:4
4 He that speaketh in an unknown tongue edifieth himself . . . .

There is one phase of speaking with tongues in our prayer life that is not praying for someone else; it is not interceding for anyone else. It is purely a means of personal spiritual edification. It aids us spiritually. It edifies us. It builds us up. We all need this kind of praying. We cannot help others; we cannot edify others unless we ourselves have been edified.

Take time to build yourself up by praying much in the Holy Spirit—with other tongues.

Spiritual things are similar to natural things. Jesus used natural things to explain spiritual things.

In the natural, no one will be expert and keen in any area without working at it. In baseball, for instance, the good hitter did not get into his position without batting practice.

Likewise, things of the spirit don't fall on us like ripe cherries off a tree. We will not be expert in spiritual things unless we take time.

Praying in the spirit will help you to be keen to spiritual things.

Praying in the Spirit
To Rest

ISAIAH 28:11,12
11 For with stammering lips and another tongue will he speak to this people.
12 To whom he said, This is the rest wherewith ye may cause the weary to rest; and this is the refreshing . . . .

Praying in the spirit and speaking in tongues is a rest.

Speaking in tongues is a continual experience to assist us in the worship of God. It is a flowing stream that should never dry up. It will enrich your life spiritually. And it will enable you to help others and to work with God Himself in the consummation of His work in the earth through the ministry of intercessory prayer.

Chapter 16

Quiet Intercession

One year my two children, Ken and Pat, studied by correspondence and my family traveled with me. We had a 43 feet long by 8 feet wide mobile home which we pulled with a pickup truck.

We were in California for a series of meetings when I was awakened suddenly in the night. I got up and checked the trailer doors thinking someone had come into the house. They were locked.

I checked Pat. She was sleeping soundly. I checked Ken. He was asleep. I came back to our bedroom and my wife was sleeping soundly.

So I lay down and began to pray in other tongues. I wasn't loud about it, but I did make expression to it.

The Bible speaks about not disturbing others in a church service. *"If any man speak in an unknown tongue, let it be by two, or at the most by three, and that by course; and let one interpret. But if there be no interpreter, let him keep silence in the church; and let him speak to himself, and to God"* (1 Cor. 14:27,28).

In other words, let him not speak out loud, but speak to himself and to God. You can sit there and talk to yourself and God without disturbing anyone. You can either whisper quietly, or you can pray on the inside of you.

That night, I did make audible sounds, but it was more of a whisper.

I began to look on the inside of me. And I picked up from my own spirit—my spirit is indwelled by the Holy Spirit and it knows things—that something was wrong with someone in my family.

I said, "Who is it, Lord? What's wrong?"

Then by an inward intuition—not a voice, but by the inward intuition that every Christian ought to have, for as many as are led by the Spirit of God they are the sons of God, and His Spirit bears witness with our spirit—I knew some family member's physical life was in danger.

I said, "Lord, I don't know who it is. I don't know for what to pray as I ought. But I'm going to trust the Holy Spirit to help me to make intercession." I lay there and prayed for nearly an hour in other tongues.

Then I had a note of victory. I knew that whatever I was praying for or about was settled. Very quietly, I sang in tongues, and laughed, then fell back to sleep.

Now this doesn't happen very often, but just before I woke up the next morning, I had a dream.

(God does speak to you in dreams sometimes. But let me say this lest folks get confused. Every time I've ever had a dream in which God spoke to me, the minute I awoke, I knew exactly what He was saying to me. If you think God spoke to you in a dream and you've got to run all over the country to find somebody to interpret it, forget it. It wasn't God. God is an intelligent being. You are an intelligent being. If He can't get over to you what He's trying to say to you, forget it. Some people think every little dream they have is God trying to say something to them. And they're in confusion all the time, trying to figure out something.)

In this dream I knew I was in Shreveport, Louisiana. I was standing outside a hotel; I saw the sign giving the name of the hotel.

Suddenly, I was inside the hotel. My younger brother was there. (Now although he had been saved and even filled with the Spirit, he was backslidden and wasn't living for God.) I saw that he took sick after midnight, in the early hours of morning.

He called the desk to tell them he was sick. Then he passed out. I saw an ambulance with red lights flashing come to take him to the hospital.

The scene changed. I was standing up against the wall in the corridor of a hospital. Across the hall there was a door. It was closed, but I knew my brother was behind it, and I knew a doctor was with him.

The doctor came out and shut the door behind him. He did not look up at me, but walked up in front of me and said, "He's dead."

In the dream, I said, "No, he's not."

Then the doctor looked up at me and said, "Well, I know better. I've pronounced too many people dead. He's dead."

I said, "No, he's not."

He said, "How do you know?"

I said, "The Lord Jesus told me."

"Oh," he said, "you're one of those nuts. I'll just show you."

He whirled around and opened the door. I followed him inside. A body lay on the table with a sheet pulled over it.

The doctor jerked the sheet down and said, "Just look!"

We looked. And my brother batted his eyes! The doctor looked closer. My brother was breathing.

The doctor looked at me and said, "You must have known something I didn't know."

I said, "I surely did."

I woke up knowing that was what I had interceded for.

That happened in May. We went on preaching in California and finished in August. At the end of August we returned to our home in Texas, after having been gone 15 months.

We hadn't been back home 15 minutes—in fact, Ken and I were still parking the trailer in the back yard—when my brother pulled into the drive.

He said to me, "I almost died while you were gone."

I said, "Yes, I know. It was last May, wasn't it?"

"Yes."

I said, "You were in Shreveport in a hotel. You took sick in the night. You called the operator, then passed out. They rushed you to the hospital. You were unconscious. The doctor told you afterwards that he thought for a while you were dead, didn't he?"

"Yes," he said. "Who told you? Momma?"

I said, "No. I haven't seen Momma. I haven't seen anyone. We just drove in here 20 minutes ago."

He said, "How did you know?"

I told him my experience.

He said, "That's exactly what happened."

Thank God for praying in tongues! This kind of praying belongs to us. This kind of praying is important. It is important to our own spiritual and physical lives. It is important in intercession for others and for the work of God in the earth. And it doesn't just belong to preachers.

Sometimes people feel that because they have to be so quiet about praying in certain places that it is not as expressive, or not as good, or not as powerful, or not as productive as otherwise. But it is.

I pray in tongues on airplanes. I pray very quietly, but it edifies me. It does something for my spirit. Now, I'm not usually interceding for anyone, but just worshiping God and building myself up spiritually. Even though I do it quietly, it is effective.

Likewise, my intercessory prayer for my brother was just as effective as I lay there on the bed beside my wife, that night in California, praying so quietly it did not disturb her.

Another time, we were preaching in Oregon. In the nighttime I was awakened. I thought I heard a door slam. Just my wife and I were in a smaller travel trailer this time. I got up and checked the doors; they were locked.

I lay back down and began to check inside my spirit. I knew prayer was needed, but I had no kind of intuition as to who or what it was.

I said, "Lord, I don't know what it is. But whatever it is, or whoever it is, somebody needs help. You said in Romans 8:26 that the Spirit helps us. So help me to make intercession."

I laid there and prayed very quietly for almost two hours. My wife slept right on by my side. Then I began to laugh and sing in tongues. I had a note of victory. I knew that whatever it was, I had the victory. I fell off to sleep.

I had no dream this time. I had no idea what it was.

Three days later someone came from the trailer park office saying we had an emergency long distance telephone call.

It was my sister calling from Texas. At first she was crying so I couldn't understand what she was saying. Finally I got her quietened down so I could tell what it was.

She said that Dub, our older brother, had broken his back. A woman had called her from a hospital in Kansas. The woman's husband was in the same room with Dub and he was going home. She was concerned that no one was there to see after Dub. He'd had an accident. He was in a cast because of the broken back and he was in a very low state physically. The doctors said they did not know if he was going to make it or not.

Oleta said, "I'm going to try to go up there, but I can't

stay. What are we going to do? Can you come?"

I realized that was what I'd been praying about. And I knew I had the answer. How did I know? I just knew. I didn't have any witness, but I just knew.

I said, "Oleta, just forget it. Don't even go up there to see about him. He's going to make it. His back will be all right. I've already got the answer. In fact, he'll be home in a few days."

And that's what happened. With the doctors telling him he couldn't do it, Dub got up three days later and went to Texas. He was in our home when we got back.

I didn't even know for whom I was praying that night— but the Spirit of God knew.

I did know that I was to pray.

Now I wake up every night and spend time talking in tongues. But I'm not praying about anybody else. I'm just fellowshiping with the Lord. I'm just communing with the Lord. I'm just worshiping the Lord. I'm just edifying my spirit. I'm just building myself up. But when I am awakened to make intercession, whether or not I know what it is about, I know it.

Usually, I lie there quietly and intercede as I have shown you.

Some have asked, "Can you pray in tongues through your mind and never say anything?"

Actually, that's not praying in tongues—that's thinking in tongues.

You have to *say* it to pray. You may say it within yourself, but it isn't saying it in your mind, it is saying it in your *spirit*.

You may say it very quietly, but you are still saying it. And it is effective.

Chapter 17

Not-So-Quiet Intercession

There are times of intercession that you are almost forced into saying it out loud. Such pressure builds up within, it seems like if you don't say it, you will burst.

My wife and I married in November 1938. I pastored a little Full Gospel church. They had no parsonage. I'd been renting a room and boarding with one of the members.

My father-in-law, a farmer in the community, said, "When you get married, move in here. We've got plenty of room and you won't have to pay room and board. This will help you get started in life."

Four days after we were married, I moved my belongings into their big farmhouse.

About 9:30 that night, my father-in-law said, "Let's have family prayer."

They were Methodists. They were attending the Full Gospel church when I came to pastor it, but they were not "Pentecostal."

We all prayed out loud in English. They weren't very loud. And I was trying to be quiet.

I kept having an "urge" to pray in tongues and I didn't know whether or not they would like that. But it just kept building, and building, and building inside me, until finally I just threw caution to the wind, lifted my voice and prayed aloud in other tongues as hard and fast as I could.

I kept my eyes tightly shut because I didn't want to see them. I just went after it. I groaned and talked in tongues.

I know I could have kept from it to begin with, but once you yield to the Spirit, then it seems like you almost can't help it.

After about 45 minutes of praying that way, the Lord

spoke to me. Only I didn't know it was the Lord.

You see, I'd been filled with the Holy Spirit less than two years. And all they taught us in Pentecostal circles in those days was, get saved and baptized with the Holy Ghost. Then they turned you loose. We just had to stumble upon anything beyond that.

But I realize now that it was the Lord who spoke these words to me, "Lay your hand on your wife and I'll fill her with the Holy Ghost."

I thought, *Well, what if I were to lay my hand on her and nothing happened?*

So I just kept praying, thinking that would go away.

Again it came, "Lay your hand on your wife and I'll fill her with the Holy Ghost."

I ignored it and went on praying.

The third time, "Lay your hand on your wife and I'll fill her with the Holy Ghost."

I opened my eyes and looked at my father-in-law kneeling to my right, and then to my wife, kneeling to my left, and then to my mother-in-law, on the other side of my wife.

I know what I said is unbelief, but God will put up with a little unbelief in you when you don't know any better. But you can't get by with that later on. This was new to me.

I said, "It won't hurt to try it."

Then I reached my left hand out and laid it on top of her head.

She had no instructions. She never sought the baptism in the Holy Spirit a day in her life. I didn't tell her to do anything. I just laid my hand on top of her head and the minute I touched her, she lifted both hands automatically and started talking fluently in tongues.

I looked at my watch to see what time it was. She

talked in tongues an hour and a half and sang three songs in other tongues. We had Pentecost in that Methodist home!

About midnight the Spirit of God spoke to me in the same voice and told me how to deal with my mother-in-law and she'd be healed. She had a double goiter. She had her suitcase packed to enter the hospital the next morning to undergo surgery.

She had no faith for healing. That is obvious. She wouldn't have had her suitcase packed to go to the hospital if she expected to be healed.

But the Spirit of the Lord told me what to do and that she'd be healed.

I did. He did. And she was. She never had the operation.

I realized afterwards what actually happened that night. What I was doing in the spirit was making intercession for my wife and for my mother-in-law.

The Spirit of God gave me intercession first. I was interceding for them. I prayed as hard and fast as I could in other tongues and with groanings for from 45 to 50 minutes. I concluded by singing in tongues and laughing in the spirit. About that time is when the Lord by the Spirit said, "Lay your hand on your wife and I'll fill her." Then He told me how to deal with my mother-in-law and that part of the goiter on the outside went down like you'd stuck a pin in a balloon.

Chapter 18
Boldness

Let us therefore come BOLDLY unto the throne of grace, that we may obtain mercy, and find grace to help in time of need.

—Hebrews 4:16

Effective intercession involves boldness.
We come before God's throne with boldness.
Where do we get boldness? In Jesus!

EPHESIANS 3:11,12
11 According to the eternal purpose which he purposed in Christ Jesus our Lord:
12 In whom we have boldness and access with confidence by the faith of him.

There are many things you do not need to pray for—but it is all right to pray for boldness. You should, in fact.

For example, you do not need to pray for faith. The Bible says, *" . . . faith cometh by hearing and hearing by the word of God"* (Rom. 10:17).

So you know how to get faith. Faith is increased by feeding it on God's Word and by exercising it. We do not need to pray for faith.

But the Bible does show us that we can pray for boldness.

Peter and John were bold when they used the Name of Jesus to minister to the lame man at the gate called Beautiful. They were bold when they proclaimed the Name of Jesus to the crowd that gathered.

The Jewish authorities noticed their boldness and took them in for questioning (Acts 4:13). They commanded them to preach and teach no more in the Name of Jesus.

Being let go, they went to their own company and reported all the chief priests and elders had said to them. Then the whole company of believers lifted up their voice with one accord in prayer unto God.

> **ACTS 4:29,30**
> 29 And now, Lord, behold their threatenings: and grant unto thy servants, that WITH ALL BOLDNESS they may speak thy word,
> 30 By stretching forth thine hand to heal; and that signs and wonders may be done by the name of thy holy child Jesus.

That prayer was answered!

> **ACTS 4:31**
> 31 And when they had prayed, the place was shaken where they were assembled together; and they were all filled with the Holy Ghost, and they spake the word of God with BOLDNESS.

Paul asked the church at Ephesus to pray for him. This great man of God, this apostle of faith, this man who wrote half the New Testament, said, *"Praying always . . . for all the saints; And for me, that utterance may be given unto me, that I may open my mouth BOLDLY, to make known the mystery of the gospel, For which I am an ambassador in bonds: that therein I may speak BOLDLY, as I ought to speak"* (Eph. 6:18-21).

The Ephesians' prayer for Paul would have been an intercessory prayer.

Boldness to Act

We need boldness to act. Sometimes during intercession the Holy Spirit may bid us to go to the one we are interceding for. I now refer to an incident in the life of a great intercessor, Charlie Hollandsworth of Spokane. One day he entered into intercession for someone. He did not know for whom he was interceding. After a time of agonizing in the Spirit he was bidden of the Spirit to go to the Monroe Street Bridge. He hurried to the bridge without delay. As he arrived, in the middle of the bridge the Holy Spirit pointed out a man with one leg over the railing ready to jump to his death. Charlie stopped the car quickly and grabbed the man. He persuaded the man to get into his car.

He drove the man out into the country where they could be alone. It took between two and three hours to get the man to accept the Lord Jesus as His Saviour.

—Reidt

We may not know for what to pray . . . But, thank God, the Holy Spirit does. We need boldness to act on God's Word. We need boldness to act on what the Spirit of God may say to us.

I can sense the Spirit of God searching through the Church trying to find intercessors whom He can trust to pray and to act with boldness. He needs them.

Many people have jobs and duties which do not allow them to give themselves wholeheartedly to intercession. Yet I have found that as you go about doing whatever you have to do, on the inside of you, you can be praying.

God will not lay a burden of intercession upon you unless you are available to move. He might move on you to pray for someone while you are working if the work is such that you can pray.

—Reidt

There are jobs where it would be very difficult for you to pray while working. So God would have to seek out someone else.

But there are some jobs—particularly if you are not

working with your mind, but with your hands, etc.—
where you could give yourself to prayer even while you're
working.

Don't throw off that burden to pray when it comes. Be
bold to act on it.

One day while I was still pastoring, I was driving along
attending to some business and visiting people. Suddenly,
I had an urge to pray for my younger brother. He was
backslidden at the time and was not walking with the
Lord. An alarm went off within me.

So I went along praying on the inside of me, even while
I was talking to other people—on the inside of me
something was reaching out to God on his behalf.

I carried that thing around with me two or three days
until it just lifted. I didn't know what it concerned.

Later on, in conversation, my brother said to me, "I'll
tell you one thing, the Lord sure helped me the other day."

He is a businessman, but he owned a ranch. He told me
how he was out on the ranch when a 5-gallon can of
gasoline he was holding in his hand exploded. He was not
the least bit hurt.

He said everyone who saw it was amazed.

The ranch manager said, "That beats anything I ever
saw in my life. I can't believe what I saw."

But three days before it happened, I was praying. I am
satisfied that if I had thrown that off and not yielded to it,
he could have been severely burned and perhaps killed.

You see, God didn't want him to leave here in that
backslidden condition.

What if I hadn't prayed?

What if Charlie Hollandsworth hadn't been responsive
to the Spirit of God? What if he hadn't interceded when he
didn't know who he was interceding for? What if he had

been too busy, or unresponsive to the leading of the Spirit to rush out to that bridge not even knowing why he was going?

In all probability, that man would have been in hell.

It's a sobering thought that when men come before the judgment bar of God, there may be some people in hell who will point to us and say, "You are responsible."

Boldness Before the Throne

ISAIAH 43:25,26
25 I, even I, am he that blotteth out thy transgressions for mine own sake, and will not remember thy sins.
26 Put me in remembrance: let us plead together: declare thou, that thou mayest be justified.

Here is a challenge from the covenant-keeping God to Israel. It is also a challenge to the Church. For if God kept His covenant with them, He will keep His covenant with us.

The believer has covenant rights in prayer, as well as other covenant rights.

Yet there is one outstanding problem that defeats believers in their prayer life. When we come to God, we have a feeling of inferiority, a sense of sin-consciousness, because we know we have failed. We have a guilt complex.

Some begin their prayers with, "I'm so weak and unworthy," and then harp on it throughout the prayer.

And when they come into the presence of God telling Him that, they talk themselves out of faith and into condemnation.

They don't know whether God hears them or not. All they do is beg for crumbs.

But look at what God said. *"I, even I, am he that blotteth*

*out thy transgressions for mine own sake, and will not
remember thy sins."*

Why did he say He would blot out our transgressions?
For His own sake—so He could bless us. He couldn't have
blessed us without it.

When we know that He blotted out our sin, that He
doesn't even remember that we ever did anything wrong,
we can come to Him with confidence. We can come with
faith. We lose sin-consciousness—and now we have Son-
consciousness!

We don't have to sit on a curbstone out in front of our
mansion, begging for favors. We can come in boldly
through the front door and enter the throne room to
fellowship with Him.

We are sons of God. We are joint heirs with Jesus
Christ. We are covenant people. We have a legal right. A
Gospel right. A son right. A family right. A Body right to
enter the throne room.

When Jesus went into the presence of the Father, He
didn't go in with just His head, leaving His little finger
outside saying, "Oh, I'm embarrassed." No! He didn't have
any condemnation even in His little finger.

We are the Body of Christ. That means the Body can go
into the presence of God the Father with the same
confidence and the same assurance that the Head can!
Boldly!

Chapter 19

Fervency

JAMES 5:16,17 *(Worrell)*
16 . . . A righteous man's inwrought supplication avails much.
17 Elijah was a man of like nature with us; and he prayed earnestly that it might not rain, and it rained not on the earth for three years and six months; and again he prayed, and the heaven gave rain, and the earth brought forth its fruit.

Effective intercession involves fervency.

The Bible teaches that we are always to be *"fervent in spirit"* (Rom. 12:11).

W. E. Vine says the word translated "fervent" in Romans 12:11 means, to be hot, to boil. Strong's Concordance adds that figuratively it means to be earnest.

Epaphrus was "laboring fervently" for the Colossians in prayers (Col. 4:12). The Greek word AGONIZOMAI translated "laboring fervently" indicates a striving, a wrestling. Ephesians 6:12 is a part of this struggle.

Chapter 20
Desire

*God . . . comforted us by the coming of Titus;
And not by his coming only, but by the consolation wherewith he was comforted in you,
when he told us your EARNEST DESIRE, your
mourning, your FERVENT mind toward me; so
that I rejoiced the more.*

—2 Corinthians 7:6,7

The Corinthians' "earnest desire" was recognized by
Titus and conveyed to Paul.

Something happens when the real God-cry, the real
God-prayer, and the real God-yearning gets a hold of our
spirit.

God lays it on your heart to intercede, then this [burden,
or whatever it is God has laid on your heart] should be the
paramount issue of your heart.

When the desire to see the answer come is intensified so
that it absorbs all the energies, then the time for the
fulfillment is not far away.

This is the desire that brings the answer. It is creative
desire.

—Reidt

In the winter of 1942 and 1943, I found myself taken up
with a desire for God to move. I did not conjure it up—it
was put there, no doubt, by God.

You see, what is happening in the move of the Spirit of
God—revivals and so forth—doesn't come as the result of
somebody's praying yesterday or even last week. It is the
result of the intercessions of yesteryear.

That winter of '42 and '43 I was pastor of a church in
East Texas when I found myself so taken up, and so
burdened, praying along certain lines.

During those war years it seemed as though many of
our churches dried up. People were busy going to war, or
working in war plants, and so forth. In our Pentecostal
churches we had an abundance of tongues and inter-
pretations, but seldom, if ever, did we see any other gifts or
manifestations of the Spirit.

I found myself almost unconsciously praying, "Dear
Lord, may the more mighty gifts and manifestations of the
Spirit come into manifestation and operation . . . the gift
of special faith . . . the working of miracles . . . the gifts of
healings . . . . "

I was so taken up with that, I would wake up in the
living room on my knees at 3 or 4 o'clock in the morning
praying that. Night after night, it was a common
occurrence. Many times I would have been awakened
earlier in the night. I'd get out of the bedroom so I wouldn't
disturb my wife. (I do a lot of praying quietly and
privately, but I couldn't be quiet about this. It seemed as if
I were going to burst.) But other times, I wouldn't
remember getting up. I would come awake and say to
myself, *How did I get here?*

I would awake and find myself unconsciously praying,
"May these greater, more mighty manifestations of your
Spirit come into operation . . . . "

Then on the 23rd day of February 1943, after praying
that day for 5 hours and 45 minutes, God began to say
something to me. I got my pencil and wrote it down. He
said, "At the close of World War II, there will come a
revival of divine healing to America."

That was more than two years before the war was over.
The war wasn't over until August 1945; this happened in
1943.

Nineteen months later, in September 1944, I was

speaking at a Christ's Ambassadors Rally for the Assemblies of God. I started out on another subject, but because this was burning inside me, I got over on this subject and told what the Lord had said to me.

I said, "I want to give you a preview of what is going to happen when the war is over. There is coming a revival of divine healing to America."

When I said that, the power of God fell on that crowd. Every minister, just like somebody told them to (and I did not), got up and ran to the altar. Every person hit the floor. I had never seen such a sight in my life.

Thank God for the Spirit of God. Thank God for prayer.

That revival of divine healing came. It started in 1947. But it didn't come because somebody had prayed the week before in 1947. It came because people—not just me, but others—were praying back in 1943.

When I was praying about it, it was a consuming desire. I did not care or even suspect that God would use me in it. I didn't really even want Him to use me. It would suit me just fine if I was behind the scenes where I could pray and nobody ever saw me.

God carries out His will upon the earth through the Church.

What if people had not responded to that burden?

Where did it come from, anyhow? Did we conjure it up ourselves? No! God laid it on our hearts. It was a consuming desire.

What if we hadn't responded? We didn't have to. We're not robots.

God doesn't *make* us do anything. We have a will of our own. We have to will to respond to the Spirit of God. God's Spirit doesn't use force. If He did, He'd make everybody get saved today and we'd go into the Millennium tomorrow.

It is the devil and demons that drive, and force, and make people.

The Holy Spirit leads and guides; He will give a gentle push.

Be determined to respond to the Spirit of God. Respond to those *urges* to pray. Sometimes there is a *leading*; sometimes there is a *burden*.

Become sensitive to Him.

Sometimes we're insensitive to what He's saying in our spirits, because we live too much in the mental realm. And we pass by these things.

> Some may object to having something become the supreme desire of the heart for a time. They say your supreme desire should be for the Lord.
>
> —Reidt

When God lays that desire on your heart, that is your supreme desire for the Lord. God dwells in you. And He is the One who activates the desire. It is God's supreme desire for people to be delivered.

It was God's supreme desire that that man not jump off the bridge and commit suicide. The man happened to be where God could find someone to start praying—someone close enough to respond to the Spirit of God and get in his car and drive out there. The man's life was saved and he was born again, because a child of God let God's supreme desire become his supreme desire.

> God is not halfhearted about anything. Since it is His supreme desire, it also becomes the supreme desire of the one called on to intercede. It is cooperation with God. "For we are labourers together with God . . . . " (1 Cor. 3:9).
>
> —Reidt

Chapter 21

Perseverance

Praying always with all prayer and supplication in the Spirit, and watching thereunto with all perseverance and supplication for all saints.

—Ephesians 6:18

Effective intercessory prayer must have in it the element of perseverance. Wilford Reidt sums it up well:

> When the Holy Spirit lays it upon a person's heart to intercede, the intercession should not stop until the answer is given or the burden lifted. In my experience where for the most part I do not know for whom I am interceding, I have had burdens last for hours and even days. I had to do usual work, but all the time there was that inner groaning in my spirit. The times when I had opportunity to get alone with God, the burden intensified. There is no rule to follow. Each person will do as God directs.
>
> The reason "persistence" is an ingredient of intercession is that it is easy to throw off a burden and forget it. It is an awesome responsibility to feel that someone's life may depend on your intercession. Not many believers are willing to accept it. So those that are willing are usually kept very busy.

Chapter 22

Intercession Against Sin

And lest, when I come again, my God will
humble me among you, and that I shall bewail
many which have sinned already, and have not
repented of the uncleanness and fornication and
lasciviousness which they have committed.
— 2 Corinthians 12:21

We have already seen that we are to travail in birth
again when necessary for Christ to be formed in believers.

Paul here said that he would "bewail" many who have
sinned and have not repented. We need to make intercession for those who have sinned and not repented.

Corinth was one of the most licentious and immoral
cities in that part of the world. The same spirits that
prevailed in the city got into the church. When Paul
named uncleanness, fornication, and lasciviousness, he
was talking about sexual impurities. People in the church
had done these things and had not repented.

The Greek word translated "bewail" means to grieve—
the feeling or the act. Here it includes both the feeling and
the act. The act being a response in intercessory prayer.

Worrell's translation sheds light on Paul's meaning.

2 CORINTHIANS 12:21 *(Worrell)*
21 Lest, when I come again, my God should humble me
before you, and I should mourn for many of those who
have heretofore sinned, and repented not of the
uncleanness, and fornication and lasciviousness
which they practiced.

We live in a world and an age of permissiveness and

immorality. Many things such as homosexuality, living together without marriage, and all uncleanness along these lines have come out of hiding.

The Church seems to have winked at some of these things. But we are to feel toward sin just like God does.

> Sin is a violation of the will of God. God is perpetually at war with sin. We use sin in its broad form that includes iniquity and transgression (1 John 3:4; 5:17). Sin leads to death (James 1:13-15). Death is separation from God. We are not talking of physical death.
>
> Sin is a hideous thing. Some men of God have expressed their feelings about it in strong language. Chrysostom (347-407 A.D.) said, "I preach and think it is more bitter to sin against Christ than to suffer the torments of hell." Anselem (11th century) said, "If hell were on one side, and sin on the other, I would rather leap into hell than willingly sin against my God."
>
> Where are the heroes, "Who resist unto blood, striving against sin?" (Heb. 12:4).
>
> . . . We only know God's estimate of sin by the magnitude of the sacrifice He has provided to atone for it, His Son!
>
> —Reidt

2 CORINTHIANS 5:10,11

10 For we must all appear before the judgment seat of Christ; that every one may receive the things done in his body, according to that he hath done, whether it be good or bad.
11 Knowing therefore the terror of the Lord, we persuade men . . . .

God is love. I preach faith—and faith works by love—so I have to preach love. But if we are not careful, we preach in such a manner that people forget God is also a God of judgment. He is also a God of justice. Sin has a penalty.

Paul grieved over the Corinthian Christians who had sinned and had not repented. No wonder. We should be grieved for those among us who are in the same situation.

Wilford Reidt said, "The awfulness of sin and its consequences should cause us to intercede for men."

Then, too, in the category of sin, God supplied a list in Revelation 21:8. He listed fear and unbelief at the top of the list—even before murder.

Seeing our brethren caught up in these snares of fear, unbelief, doubt, unforgiveness, worry, and so forth should compel us to intercede for them.

Chapter 23

Intercession for Deliverance

> *Finally, brethren, pray for us that the word of the Lord may have free course, and be glorified, even as it is with you: AND THAT WE MAY BE DELIVERED from unreasonable and wicked men: for all men have not faith. But the Lord is faithful, who shall stablish you, and keep you from evil.*
>
> —2 Thessalonians 3:1-3

"Pray for us that we may be delivered . . . ."

The Thessalonicans carrying out Paul's prayer request would have been interceding for another—for Paul—for his deliverance and protection.

Many are the accounts I know of first hand—some from our own experience and others from people we know—where because of intercession people were delivered.

Wilford Reidt knew personally a mother God awakened at 2 o'clock in the morning to pray for her son. She knew from the urgency of the Spirit that something was seriously wrong. She did not quench that urgency, but yielded to it. She earnestly gave herself to intercession until the burden lifted. Later she learned that at the moment God called her to intercede, the ship her son was on was struck by lightning. The medics on the warship laid her son out for dead—and put his body with others in a place for the dead. He surprised them some time later by reviving. He is alive today because his mother prayed.

I heard Brother T., an old-time Pentecostal minister and missionary, tell something that happened when he and his wife, Blanche, were in Africa as missionaries.

His wife's parents lived on a farm in the New England states. Her father had been an unsaved alcoholic, dying with cirrhosis of the liver, when he was carried into one of Sister Woodworth-Etter's meetings and marvelously healed, saved, and filled with the Holy Spirit.

At the time of this happening, his daughter and son-in-law were in Africa as missionaries. Before sunup one morning he headed for the barn to milk the cows. Halfway between the barn and the house at about 5 o'clock, he set down the milk pails and came back into the kitchen.

His wife looked up from cooking breakfast. "What's wrong? You look pale. Are you sick?"

He said, "No, I'm not sick."

She said, "What's the matter?"

He said, "I don't know what it is, but something's wrong with Blanche. Her life is in danger. Let's pray."

He fell down on the kitchen floor and began to groan in the spirit and pray with tongues.

Six o'clock came. He still was praying.

Seven o'clock came. He still was praying.

Eight o'clock. The cows were lowing. The chicks were cackling; the pigs were squealing; they hadn't been fed. Still he prayed, groaning and agonizing.

Nine o'clock. Ten o'clock. Eleven o'clock. Old Brother G., 82 years old, still hadn't gotten up from the floor.

Twelve o'clock. One o'clock. He still prayed.

Two o'clock in the afternoon. Nine hours without stopping, groaning, crying, and praying. Then at two o'clock the burden lifted. He laughed and sang in tongues.

"Whatever it is," he said to his wife praying with him, "we've got it!"

Communications were not what they are today. In the process of time, a letter came by boat from Africa.

I heard Brother T. tell what he'd written in that letter.

"I wrote to tell them that Blanche contracted a tropical fever," he said.

It was one that when you got it, you did not survive.

He told how Blanche had indeed gone right down to the place of death. In fact, she was left for dead. But suddenly, she rose up well!

Eventually, they compared notes. Allowing for the difference in time, the exact time she rose up well was at 2 o'clock, when the burden left her father.

He had wrestled with it nine hours. That's persistence. He had refused to give up until the burden lifted.

Now—here is something many have missed. *God help us to see it.*

Let me say it again, we emphasize faith and the prayer of faith endeavoring to get people to believe God "now" for their own individual healing. But we do not mean to leave the impression that that is the only kind of praying.

In crusades and seminars, for example, we endeavor to get people to the position of faith right now to receive their own immediate needs. We are dealing with people who are there for their own individual needs.

The laws that govern the operation of the prayer of faith do not govern the operation of the prayer of intercession.

The prayer of faith is prayed primarily for yourself.

It is not often you can pray the prayer of faith for someone else—unless they are bona fide baby Christians. You can carry them temporarily on your faith, in some instances.

If Brother G. had not known something about intercession—if he had simply heard about the prayer of faith, which is right and legitimate—he might have said to his wife, "We don't know what it is. But whatever it is, let's just agree that she'll be all right."

That would not have worked. She would have died.

The prayer of faith doesn't always work in every situation. It isn't designed to—if it were, that would be the only prayer we'd ever need to pray. We wouldn't need all the other kinds of praying that the Spirit of God through the Word encourages people to pray.

I can always pray the prayer of faith for myself. And I do that. But I cannot always pray the prayer of faith for the other fellow.

Sometimes I can—if I can get him to agree with me. If he is not present, how can I get him to agree with me?

Great victories have been won through intercession.

Great battles have been lost because we did not take time to intercede.

In 1965 I preached a six-week meeting in Oklahoma. Then I drove back to my home near Dallas to take care of some business before driving to Kansas City to speak at a Full Gospel Business Men's banquet.

When I got home I had a burden to pray for someone. I had the sensation of someone's being thrown from an automobile. But I had so much business to attend to in a short time that I got to thinking, *I've got to do this, and that, and the other,* and I let it slip by me.

I did pray silently. But I should have taken time to really get quiet and alone with God to find out, *Why is this coming to me? What is this?* I should have taken time to get over into the spirit out beyond the natural.

It was raining when we left Dallas on Friday. We had seat belts in the car, but I never wore them. This time, I fastened my seat belt.

My wife said, "What is it?" She knew I never did that.

I said, "I don't know. I had the sensation of someone's

being thrown out of the car, and I thought it might be us."

We prayed in a general way and claimed protection.

We spent the night in Tulsa with friends. When we left on Saturday morning, it still was raining.

Again, I fastened my seat belt because I couldn't get away from that sensation. I should have taken time to pray about it, but I did not.

We were in Kansas City on Saturday night, actually eating the banquet just before I was to speak, when someone came with the message that I had a long distance phone call.

I went to the phone. Our son told me that my niece had had an accident and was thrown through the windshield. The doctors didn't give her a chance to live.

That's what God was trying to tell me.

We talk about the times we listened—but there are times we did not. Why hadn't I taken the time? I was too busy to assume the responsibility.

What an awesome responsibility. Lives oftentimes hinge on our praying.

What would have happened if I had taken the time to intercede? She would have avoided that accident.

What did happen? She died at 25 leaving two children, ages 3 and 5.

In 1939 my wife and I had accepted another pastorate and had moved away, but we were back in the area where we'd first lived, visiting her parents.

We went with them to visit a neighboring farmer. He'd been sickly, but they hadn't discovered exactly what was wrong. They knew it was serious.

The women were in the house. This man, my father-in-law, and myself were sitting on the front porch, talking.

On the inside of me, I had a burden, an agony really, to

pray for the man. As he and my father-in-law talked, the
man opened the door by something he said for me to move
right in. But I didn't. I held my peace. Then the
conversation changed. And I never could work it around
again. I said nothing to him about his spiritual welfare.

We spent another day or two with my wife's folks, then
came on home. A couple of days later, my mother-in-law
called and said this man had died.

I regretted for a while that I hadn't followed up on the
leading of the Lord and said something to him. Then I
thought no more about it.

Sunday night, as was our custom, we met at the altar to
pray 15 minutes before the service.

I stepped off the platform, knelt, and had just shut my
eyes when I was in the Spirit. I saw that man. I shall never
forget it. It took me weeks to get away from it. I'd wake up
in the night and see it. I saw this man in hell. I saw the
fires of hell boiling up around him. I heard his screams. I
heard him cry out like the rich man did for water to cool his
tongue.

Then I saw Jesus. He pointed at me and said, "I'm going
to hold you responsible for him. I gave you a burden of
prayer and you didn't pray. I opened the door for you to
talk and you didn't talk."

"Oh, my God!" I cried. With tears, on my knees for an
hour and a half, I repented, crying, "Oh, God. Let that
thing pass from me."

I didn't preach that night. The others didn't know what
was happening.

We should never take an urge to pray lightly. It may
make the difference between life and death to some other
soldier of the cross.

—Reidt

Chapter 24
The Interceding Body

And whether one member suffer, all the members suffer with it . . . .
— 1 Corinthians 12:26

Intercessory prayer is the type of suffering that brings deliverance. We are members one of another. As the Body of Christ and as members, we should partake in the healing of each other. We weep with those who weep— then we rejoice with those who rejoice (Rom. 12:15).

ROMANS 15:1
1 We then that are strong ought to bear the infirmities of the weak, and not to please ourselves.

How do we bear the infirmities of the weak? To answer that question we must also ask for the meaning of "bear" and of "infirmities."
"Bear" means to lift with the idea of removing.
"Infirmities" means in this setting "a scruple of conscience." Therefore it is not a physical thing, but something wrong in their belief.
—Reidt

In the surrounding Scriptures, Paul discussed the fact that some people felt it was wrong to eat meat, because sometimes the blood of animals sold in the marketplace for meat had been offered to idols.

Paul said that there was only one God, and these meats were not offered to our Father God. But yet, if eating meat offered to idols would cause his brother to offend, he wouldn't eat it as long as the world stands. Then he gives Romans 15:1.

A scruple of conscience is involved. They are brothers, but they are weak.

> To help them   is necessary to engage in intercessory prayer for them.   is helps pull down the stronghold Satan has in their life   nd helps bring about their acceptance of good teaching th   ill correct the trouble.
>
> —Reidt

The Ephesian Prayers

Pray

* Ephesians 1:17-23 a d 3:14-21 are Holy Spirit-given prayers which apply to t e Church everywhere.

The turning point in my life came when I prayed them a thousand times or more for myself. I would kneel, open my Bible, and say, "Fath r, I am praying these prayers for myself. Because they are pirit-given prayers, this has to be Your will for me just as it was Your will for the Church at Ephesus . . . . "

Then I would continue ist as the prayers read except where Paul said, "you," I w uld substitute "me," like this:

> *"God, of our Lord Jesus Ch ist, the Father of glory,*
> *Give unto 'me' the spirit of   isdom and revelation in the*
> *knowledge of Him,*
> *The eyes of 'my' understandi g being enlightened;*
> *That 'I' may know what is the ope of his calling,*
> *and what the riches of the g ory of*
> *his inheritance in the saint*
> *And what is the exceeding g eatness of his power*
> *to usward who believe, acco ding to the*
> *working of his mighty powe*
> *Which he wrought in Christ, hen he raised him*
> *from the dead, and set him a is own right hand*
> *in the heavenly places . . . . "*

After about six months, the first thing I was praying for started happening. The revelation of God's Word began to come.

Now that is how those prayers worked when I prayed them for myself. The subject of this book is intercessory prayer—prayer for another. I also have used these same prayers in intercession for Christians who do not see certain Bible truths.

I pray these prayers for them every morning and night. I use their name, like this:

> "Lord, I am praying this prayer for Joe. God of our Lord, Jesus Christ, the Father of glory, give unto Joe the spirit of wisdom and revelation in the knowledge of Him: I pray that the eyes of Joe's understanding be enlightened; that Joe may know what is the hope of his calling, and what the riches of the glory of His inheritance in the saints . . . ."

. . . and so on through the two prayers.

I prayed ten days for one relative, morning and night. With no human teacher talking to him (he was a Spirit-filled Christian), he wrote me, "It's amazing how things have opened up to me. I'm beginning to see what you've been talking about."

You see, God has already blessed us with all spiritual blessings in heavenly places in Christ Jesus (Eph. 1:3). Some Christians just don't know it, so they can't take advantage of it. They suffer from the infirmity of not knowing.

We can pray these prayers in Ephesians for them. It is necessary to stay with it—morning and night, and more often if possible.

Bearing One Another's Burdens

GALATIANS 6:2
**2 Bear ye one another's burdens, and so fulfil the law
of Christ.**

Intercession is involved in bearing one another's
burdens.

Remember that "bear" means to lift with the idea of
removing. Intercessory prayer is one way we can lift with
the idea of removing burdens people are carrying.

> People may be carrying heavy burdens caused by hurts
> in the past. They may be carrying loads because of the
> willful sinning of other saints. They may have some faults
> or sins in their lives they are having trouble getting rid of.
> Burdens can be any number of things.
> They may be having trouble laying aside the weights
> (hindrances) that keep them from running a good race
> (Heb. 12:1,2). Intercessory prayer can help lift these loads
> and weights so they can run in complete freedom.
>
> —Reidt

HEBREWS 12:1,2
**1 Wherefore seeing we also are compassed about
with so great a cloud of witnesses, let us lay aside
every weight, and the sin which doth so easily beset
us, and let us run with patience the race that is set
before us,**
**2 Looking unto Jesus, the author and finisher of our
faith; who for the joy that was set before him endured
the cross, despising the shame, and is set down at the
right hand of the throne of God.**

This talks about two things which hinder Christians in
the race we are running—weights and sins. (What may be

a weight to one, may not be a weight to another.)

We can help fellow believers to run their races better by helping to lift these burdens through intercessory prayer. We don't need to criticize them; we need to pray for them.

When we take our places in intercessory prayer for each other, we are helping the entire body to come into maturity.

Chapter 25

Interceding
Against the Powers of Darkness

In the tenth chapter of Daniel, we learn that something was revealed to Daniel. He went on a partial fast, praying and seeking God. It was three full weeks, however, before an angel came with the answer Daniel was seeking.

Daniel's prayer was heard the first day he prayed, the angel told him:

> **DANIEL 10:12**
> **12 . . . from the first day that thou didst set thine heart to understand, and to chasten thyself before thy God, thy words were heard, and I am come for thy words.**

In the next verse, the angel disclosed the secret of why it took so long for Daniel's prayer to be answered: *"But THE PRINCE OF THE KINGDOM OF PERSIA WITHSTOOD ME one and twenty days: but, lo, Michael, one of the chief princes, came to help me . . . ." (v. 13).*

Let's look back at the first verse of this chapter: *"In the third year of Cyrus king of Persia a thing was revealed unto Daniel."* These events, then, are dated as having happened during the third year of the reign of Cyrus, *king* of Persia. Cyrus was a man who sat on the throne of the kingdom of Persia.

But in the 13th verse, the angel said, "the *prince* of Persia withstood me." This prince of Persia fought, up in the heavenlies, against God's message-bearing angel. Reinforcements—Michael the archangel—had to come to help the angel get through with that message to Daniel! This prince of Persia was a spirit being.

111

We see from this passage of Scripture, among others, that *there is a double kingdom system.*

There is a *seen* kingdom upon the earth with human rulers. But behind that earthly kingdom (or nation) is an *unseen* kingdom with a satanic ruler.

This explains something about the temptation of Jesus.

> **LUKE 4:5,6**
> **5 And the devil, taking him [Jesus] up into an high mountain, shewed unto him all the kingdoms of the world in a moment of time.**
> **6 And the devil said unto him, All this power will I give thee, and the glory of them: FOR THAT IS DELIVERED UNTO ME; and to whomsoever I will I give it.**

What power is being discussed here? The power of the nations of this world!

Some have suggested the devil didn't have that power or authority. If so, wouldn't Jesus have known that and told him so?

The Bible says this was a temptation. If the devil *didn't* have that power and authority, it couldn't have been a temptation—and the Son of God would have been partner to a lie and a fraud. But it was a *bona fide* temptation.

Where, then, did Satan get that authority? Did God give it to him?

God made the world and the fullness thereof. Then He made His man Adam. And this is what a lot of people—including ministers—haven't seen. God said, "Adam, I give you dominion over all the works of my hands." In one sense, God was saying, "Adam, you're the god of this world. You run it." *God gave the world to Adam!*

But the New Testament calls Satan the god of this world (Second Corinthians 4:4). When did Satan become the god of this world? When Adam sinned. It was when Adam committed high treason and sold out to Satan.

Notice what Satan said to Jesus: *"All this power will I give thee, and the glory of them* [the kingdoms of the world]: *FOR THAT IS DELIVERED UNTO ME . . . . "* Who delivered it to Satan? God didn't. Adam did.

Rulers of Darkness

The angel told Daniel, "Your prayer got through the very first day." And God hears us the first day we pray, but we do have to stand sometimes before the answer comes.

It is not God who withholds answers to our prayers—He sends the answer the minute we pray—there are forces out in the heavens endeavoring to intercept those answers.

Let's examine Ephesians 6:12. It begins, *"For we wrestle . . . . "* Who's "we"? The Church. Paul is writing to the New Testament Church—to believers everywhere.

"We wrestle not against flesh and blood . . . . " That's our trouble. We try to fight, wrestle, and cope with situations we *see*, when we're really wrestling against an unseen power behind the situation. When we understand that, we'll be successful in our "wrestling."

"We wrestle not against flesh and blood, but against principalities, against powers, AGAINST THE RULERS OF THE DARKNESS OF THIS WORLD . . . . "

Rulers of the darkness of this world! Another Scripture declares, *"the whole world lieth in wickedness"* (1 John 5:19). The *Amplified* translation reads, "and the whole world (around us) is under the power of the evil one."

If the whole world lies in wickedness and in darkness,

then the devil is ruling the whole world. The devil is ruling everybody who is unsaved. And he rules! He's not ruling us, however, because the Bible says that although we're *in* the world, we're not *of* the world. We're children of light, not darkness.

The Holy Spirit is a gentleman. He will not take any more territory than you surrender to Him. He'll not dominate you. He'll not force you.

Demons, on the other hand, use force. We read in the Bible about them driving people; forcing people.

There's something here that we need to be very careful of: *Anybody who wants to drive, force, and dominate people is motivated by the spirit of the devil.* We see it in religious circles.

"Rulers of the darkness of this world." Hold this phrase from Ephesians 6 in your mind while we turn to the Book of Colossians for a clearer picture still.

> COLOSSIANS 1:12
> 12 Giving thanks unto the Father, which hath made us meet [able] to be partakers of the inheritance of the saints in light.

Notice that expression "in light"!

Now notice the following verse: *"Who hath delivered us from the power of darkness . . . . "* The *Amplified* version reads, "[The Father] has delivered and drawn us to Himself out of the control and the dominion of darkness and has transferred us into the kingdom of the Son of His love."

You see, the Father has taken us out from under the control of darkness and the rulers of darkness—the devil, demons, and evil spirits in Satan's kingdom. This is what Ephesians 6:12 is talking about.

It says we "wrestle." We're not wrestling with God. Who do we wrestle with, then? Ephesians 6:12 says we wrestle against *"principalities, against powers, against the rulers of the darkness of this world, **against spiritual wickedness in high places**."*

A marginal note in my King James Version says, "wicked spirits in the heavenlies." Three heavens are spoken of in the Bible.

Bible scholars agree that the Apostle Paul was talking about himself in Second Corinthians 12:2 when he said, *"I knew a man in Christ above fourteen years ago, (whether in the body, I cannot tell; or whether out of the body, I cannot tell: God knoweth;) such an one caught up to the third heaven."*

The first of the three heavens, right above us, is what we call the atmospheric heaven. Beyond that, away out in space, are the stars, etc. Then out beyond that is the third heaven—the Heaven of heavens—where the throne of God is.

There are wicked spirits in the atmospheric heaven above us—"in the heavenlies." We get another glimpse of this fact in the 28th chapter of Ezekiel.

The first 10 verses are a "word of the Lord," a prophetic message, given through Ezekiel to the prince of Tyrus, who was lifted up in pride. God said to him through the Prophet Ezekiel, *"yet thou art a man."* So this prince of Tyrus was a man. Angels are not men. Evil spirits are not men.

In verses 11-19 of the same chapter, another prophetic word is given through Ezekiel, but this one is addressed to the *king* of Tyrus, a being who could not be the *prince* of Tyrus, whom God had identified earlier as a man. The king of Tyrus, therefore, must be a being, a spiritual power, a dark power, behind this kingdom.

> EZEKIEL 28:11-15
> 11 Moreover the word of the Lord came unto me, saying,
> 12 Son of man, take up a lamentation upon the king of Tyrus, and say unto him, Thus saith the Lord God; Thou sealest up the sum, full of wisdom, and perfect in beauty.
> 13 Thou hast been in Eden the garden of God; every precious stone was thy covering . . . the workmanship of thy tabrets and of thy pipes was prepared in thee in the day that thou wast created.
> 14 Thou art the anointed cherub that covereth; and I have set thee so: thou wast upon the holy mountain of God; thou hast walked up and down in the midst of the stones of fire.
> 15 Thou wast perfect in thy ways from the day that thou wast created, till iniquity was found in thee.

God was talking about the devil—Lucifer—when He said, *"Thou hast been in Eden the garden of God . . . ."* The prince of Tyrus, a man, couldn't have been there. He wasn't even born. No, this "king of Tyrus" is not a man; he is a *created* being (vv. 13,15).

In these two beings—the prince of Tyrus, a man; and the king of Tyrus, a spirit being, Lucifer himself—the Bible gives the idea of a natural kingdom upon the earth dominated by a spiritual kingdom with the same name.

Everything on this earth—every human, every being—is dominated, ruled, or influenced by spirits in the unseen world. Even we as Christians are influenced and led by the Spirit of God. Romans 8:14 says, *"For as many as are led by the Spirit of God, they are the sons of God."*

If people could ever understand about this other world—this spirit world—that exists and understand that it's the world in which God lives—a world that has no beginning or end—faith would become an easy thing; a natural thing.

The reason you can count things done before they materialize is because **they're already done in the spirit realm.** If you'll believe they're done in this realm, they will be made manifest.

That's the reason Jesus said, *"What things soever ye desire, when ye pray, believe that ye receive them, and ye shall have them"* (Mark 11:24).

Now I want you to notice something that perhaps you never noticed before. Let's go back to that sixth chapter of Ephesians:

> **EPHESIANS 6:10-18**
> 10 Finally, my brethren, be strong in the Lord, and in the power of his might.
> 11 Put on the whole armour of God, that ye may be able to stand against the wiles of the devil.
> 12 For we wrestle not against flesh and blood, but against principalities, against powers, against the rulers of the darkness of this world, against spiritual wickedness in high places.
> 13 Wherefore take unto you the whole armour of God, that ye may be able to withstand in the evil day, and having done all, to stand.
> 14 Stand therefore, having your loins girt about with truth, and having on the breastplate of righteousness;
> 15 And your feet shod with the preparation of the gospel of peace;
> 16 Above all, taking the shield of faith, wherewith ye shall be able to quench all the fiery darts of the wicked.
> 17 And take the helmet of salvation, and the sword of the Spirit, which is the word of God:
> 18 PRAYING always with all prayer and supplication in the Spirit, and watching thereunto with all perseverance and supplication for all saints.

We usually stop reading with the 17th verse. By so doing, we've taken these verses out of context. There is more truth in them than we have seen.

Because we *do* wrestle in our prayer life against principalities, powers, rulers of the darkness of this world, and wicked spirits in the heavenlies, **the object of taking on the whole armor of God is so that we can enter into the prayer life!**

Putting on the armor of God and *not* entering into the prayer conflict is practically useless!

Christians entering into prayer should never forget this fact: *We have authority in the Name of Jesus against all powers of darkness!*

In the 45 years since I learned to really pray, I've never prayed a single prayer concerning myself or my own needs without almost instantly getting the answer.

Why? Because I know how to pray. I know what belongs to me. I know how to take authority over the devil. I know how to speak to him and tell him, "Stop your maneuvers right now!"

The Bible calls us citizens of Heaven. I know how to demand *my* rights; however, I can't always demand another person's rights for him. As an American citizen I can exercise my right to vote, but I can't exercise your right to vote. You've got to do that for yourself.

Many times people run around trying to get somebody else to pray for them. It doesn't always work. That's because they don't have the authority.

Here's where intercession comes in. We have to intercede for people who don't know their rights. They may be honest, sincere, saved for years, and even filled with the Spirit, but spiritual things remain hidden to them.

When praying for others, we may have to take more
time to intercede, because they may be yielding to evil
spirits. Sometimes even Christians yield to evil spirits and
allow them to dominate them.

In praying for my own relatives, I've had to take time to
stand against the devil. I've usually prayed for my
relatives privately, secretly; I haven't said anything to
them.

(That's our trouble: We try to deal with *the individual*
when we ought to be dealing with *the power* behind the
problem.)

I've simply said, *"I break the power of the devil over
so-and-so!"*

Ephesians 6:18 speaks about making supplication "for
all saints." (You see, they don't always know how to pray
for themselves.)

An intercessor is one who takes the place of another.

Interceding in Tongues

One form of intercession is intercession in an unknown
tongue.

1 CORINTHIANS 14:14
**14 For if I pray in an unknown tongue, my spirit
prayeth, but my understanding is unfruitful.**

Praying in tongues provides a way for us to pray for
"things we know not"—for things we don't even know
about—for people we don't know.

The Spirit of God can help us make intercession for
people and situations when we don't know how we should
pray "as we ought." We know we should pray, but we don't
know *how* to pray in many cases.

I've come to that place many times. I've said, "Lord, I know to pray, but not as I ought."

Praying "God bless so-and-so," "God help them," or, "God do this," seemed inadequate. I've said, "Lord, I'm going to trust the Holy Spirit to help me make intercession for this individual or situation." And I begin to pray in other tongues.

Interceding with the Understanding

We can make intercession with our understanding for things we know about. I'm convinced we have authority and power in this area that we've never yet used. Some of us have gotten into the edge of it.

In 1947, my Sunday School superintendent, an oil field pumper, fell from on top of the pump house into the engine. The report came to me that he was dead.

When I arrived on the scene, he was lying on the ground close to the pump house. An ambulance was backed up nearby. People were all around. I knelt down beside Dr. Garrett. He whispered to me, "I thought he was dead at first. He isn't yet, but he will die soon, and we can't move him. We'll kill him if we do."

Then the doctor said, "Reverend Hagin, take his wife aside and prepare her for this."

I took her by the arm and led her to one side—not to prepare her, however, but to pray with her.

As we moved away from the crowd, she said, "Brother Hagin, Dr. Garrett doesn't think Daddy will live, does he?"

I said, "No, he doesn't, Sister."

She said, "Isn't it wonderful that you and I have inside information?" (She meant information inside the Bible!)

I said, "Yes, thank God, we do. We'll pray and he'll live."

Well, he kept on living, wrapped in blankets, lying on the ground. Dr. Garrett remained beside him. Finally he decided to risk moving him to the hospital. I think he must have sensed we were holding him there, for he said to me, "I'm sure we'll never make it to Tyler with him alive, but we'll put him in the ambulance and try. Reverend Hagin, you get in and ride with him."

To make a long story short, he did survive the trip. Three doctors were awaiting him.

I went to the hospital and sat up with him at night. His wife stayed with him day and night.

The third night about 8 o'clock, one of the doctors said to me, "Reverend, I'll be honest with you. This is the third night and he's still in shock. We don't even know the extent of his injuries. We can't take him to the X-ray room to find out. If we move him, we'll kill him. We've done everything we know to do. He's going fast now, and there just isn't anything we can do."

Back in the room I saw that the man's wife was growing tired. (The spirit is willing, but the flesh is weak. When you grow tired physically, it's difficult for your spirit, your inward man, to continue to dominate. Especially when you're looking right at the situation.) I saw her faith was waning. And I knew I had to get her out of there. I knew he would die if she stayed.

(The reason a lot of people have died is because their relatives have stayed with them! I've found out why Jesus sometimes put people out of the room when He was about to heal the sick.)

I didn't lie to her, but I didn't tell her what the doctor had told me. I said, "Now, you go rest. I'll call you if there's any change here. But he'll be all right."

I had to do some spiritual wrestling that night. As long

as I was awake and alert, my Sunday School superintendent did fine. But this was the third night I had sat up
myself, and when I'd doze off in the chair, he'd begin to die.

The special duty nurse awakened me as she walked
around the bed to check on him under the oxygen tent.
When I first looked at him, I thought, *He's dead! I've gone
to sleep and let the man die right on my hands!*

Excitedly, I asked the nurse, "Is he dead?"

"No," she said. "I thought he was. But he'll never live
till I go off duty at 7." It was 2 a.m. then.

I went out into the hall, and I prayed. Very quietly, I
interceded for him. I argued his case. You see, God said:

> **ISAIAH 43:25,26**
> **25 I, even I, am he that blotteth out thy transgressions
> for mine own sake, and will not remember thy sins.
> 26 Put me in remembrance: let us plead together:
> declare thou, that thou mayest be justified.**

"Put me in remembrance." God told us to remind Him of
what He said. This is talking about prayer. "Declare
thou." The marginal note in the King James Version
renders this "set forth your cause." In other words, God
invites us, "Plead your case."

So I simply said in a whisper at 2 a.m. out in the
hospital hallway, "Lord, I'm just not going to let him die!"
And I set forth my case in front of Him.

"Number one," I said, "he's my Sunday School
superintendent. He may not be the best one in the world,
but he's the best one I've ever had. He helps me. He visits
the absentees. He works at it all during the week. And he
helps in a number of other ways.

"Secondly, he puts 30 percent of his income into the
church.

"Thirdly, he's an influence for God and for good. I've talked to businessmen downtown. They believe in him; respect him.

"I need him. I'm the under shepherd, and You're the Great Shepherd of the Church. What I need, You need.

"Fourthly, the Bible plainly tells us death is an enemy. It's not of God. It's really of the devil. When the devil is finally eliminated, death will be eliminated from human contact. So I just rebuke death and command it to leave him. I'm not going to let him die!"

I went back into his room, sat down, and again dozed off. He started dying. I got up and went through it again, pleading his case. Actually, I went through it four times; the fourth time at 4 a.m.

At 8 o'clock, the doctor came in, pulled up the oxygen tent, and began to listen across his chest. After a little he turned to me and exclaimed, "He's come out of it! He's come out of it! You know, he might make it now! Get the stretcher! We'll take him to X-ray."

When they brought him back from X-ray, the same doctor said to me, "He's got a 50-50 chance."

I just stood there, but inside I was jumping up and down, thinking, *Fifty-fifty chance! What are you talking about, doctor? He's got a hundred percent chance to make it!* And he did make it.

Now, I never said a word to my wife or anybody else about the way I had prayed for this man. But the first time he was back in church, he testified.

First he thanked everybody for their prayers. Then he said, "Never feel sorry for anybody who dies. The last thing I remember was falling. I don't even remember hitting down in the machinery. The next conscious thing I knew was when I woke up in the hospital. And after I woke up, I never had any pain or hurt.

"But while I was unconscious, I must have died. I went up to Heaven. I heard an angelic choir. You never heard such singing in your life.

"I saw Jesus. Jesus came to me. And I was just about to fall down before Him and tell Him how much I loved Him when He said, 'You'll have to go back.'

"I said, 'I don't want to go back.'

"Jesus said, 'You'll have to go back to the earth.'

"I said, 'I don't want to go back to the earth.'

"The third time Jesus said, 'You'll have to. *Brother Hagin won't let you come.*'

"Then Jesus turned, and like you would pull a lace curtain back from a window, He pulled back a curtain and I heard Brother Hagin say, 'Lord, I'm not going to let him die.'

"Jesus said, 'See, he won't let you come.'

"The next thing I knew, I woke up in the hospital," my Sunday School superintendent concluded.

I had not told him I'd prayed that way. How did he know? The Lord let him hear me, and told him that was the reason he couldn't stay in Heaven!

That got me started thinking, 'way back there in 1947, that we have authority to make intercession which we've never used.

I believe that at times, without realizing it, we have taken our place in our covenant in the Name of Jesus and have made intercession. Without examining the Bible on the subject, we have thought, *That was a great experience the Lord helped me to have. I might not ever have another one like it.* And that kind of thinking has defeated us.

Three years later when my father-in-law lay dying in the hospital, I got to thinking about that experience with the Sunday School superintendent.

As I stood by his bedside—he was unconscious—I said, "Lord, I believe I'll just rebuke this death and command it to leave him. I believe I'll command him to live in Jesus' Name."

God said in Isaiah 43:26, "Let *us* plead *together*." On the inside of me, the Lord plainly said to me by the Spirit, "No, don't do it. Don't you do it."

That meant I had the authority to do it!

"Leave him alone and let him die," He said. And the Lord pled his case. "First, he's 70 years old. All I've promised you is 70 or 80 years." (That is a minimum. You can go longer. If you've got more faith, claim more. But don't settle for anything less.)

"Second," He said, "he's ready to go. Spiritually, financially, he's got everything ready. He hasn't always been ready. His finances are in order; all his business is in order. He'll never have a better time to die than now. So you leave him alone and let him die."

I said, "All right, Lord, I will under one condition and one condition only. Bring him out of this death; let him revive and leave a good testimony so everybody will know where he went. Then I'll let him go."

I hadn't gotten those words out of my mouth until he opened his eyes.

"Kenneth," he said, "I'm dying."

I said, "I know it, Mr. Rooker."

He said, "Now, the sooner the better."

I said, "I know that."

He said, "You're going to get those children up here and let me see them before I go, aren't you?"

I said, "Yes, sir. I'll do it."

Our children were his only grandchildren. I phoned our

pastor in Garland, Texas, and asked him to bring the children over to the hospital in Sherman. Meanwhile, I talked to the Mother Superior of this Catholic hospital and asked about bringing small children in.

She said, "Don't pay attention to any rules. That man should have been dead two days ago. We can't understand how he's lived. Bring in anybody you want to—it's just a miracle that he's revived."

So his family, including the little grandchildren, gathered around his bed. And you'd have thought he was going on a vacation the next day. He never shed a tear. The nurses rolled up the head of his bed, and he sat there laughing and talking.

The next day he lapsed into unconsciousness and started dying. I stood at the foot of the bed just as death fastened its final throes upon him.

Suddenly his eyes popped open. He saw me and said, "My God, Kenneth, I'm dying."

I said, "I know, Mr. Rooker, but you're not afraid to go."

"No," he said. "I'm not afraid."

I said, "Lie back on the pillow and let 'er go."

He lay back, smiled, relaxed, and a light flashed across his face as he took off. Praise God! (You've got to have faith to live—but you've got to have faith to die, too.)

It is possible to make intercession and get answers sometimes which are not always the wisest and the best.

We need to use wisdom—because we do have authority. I've learned that from experience. I know it from the Word.

According to the Word, many times what we say, He will do—because we've got the authority down here.

I am satisfied that if we will just walk in the light of God's Word and make intercession, we can change the lives of our loved ones and the life of our nation.

We can hold back the powers of darkness. We can undo the works of the devil.

Chapter 26

Fasting

And let it be, when these signs are come unto thee, that thou do as occasion serve thee; for God is with thee.

—1 Samuel 10:7

In some cases fasting may be necessary. There is no hard and fast rule. The prayer warrior will do as occasion shall serve him. If he deems fasting necessary, then fast.

—Reidt

In all the Epistles—the books of the New Testament written to the Church—not one time do they tell the Church to fast.

That doesn't mean we should not. Mention is made of fasting, but no rules are laid down, nor do they even encourage the Church to fast.

The reason is, there are no hard and fast rules about it—it is to be done as the occasion arises.

Fasting does not change God. He is the same before you fast, while you are fasting, and when you get through fasting.

But fasting will change you. It will help you keep the flesh under. It will help you become more susceptible to the Spirit of God.

The Lord may speak to you to fast. He has spoken to me to fast at special times. I might mention, however, that never have I been led to fast more than three days at a time.

Chapter 27

Interceding for Your Nation

I exhort therefore, that, first of all, supplications, prayers, intercessions, and giving of thanks, be made for all men; For kings, and for all that are in authority; that we may lead a quiet and peaceable life in all godliness and honesty. For this is good and acceptable in the sight of God our Saviour; Who will have all men to be saved, and to come unto the knowledge of the truth.

—1 Timothy 2:1-4

After the final service of our Campmeeting '79, some of the speakers and others went up to Kenneth Hagin Jr.'s hotel suite for sandwiches.

As we were talking about the things of God, the Spirit of God kept moving on me. (Actually, only three times in my life has the Spirit moved on me in such a measure.)

I said to the others, "Let's pray. The Spirit of God keeps moving on me."

We prayed. By the Spirit, I ministered to each one present. Then I was caught up in the spirit of prayer and intercession. For lack of a better term, I was "lost in the spirit." I was not unconscious—but I was more conscious of spiritual things. Spiritual things were more real than the natural.

I sat with my eyes shut, praying in tongues, for what proved to be several hours. (It was just after midnight when we started praying. When it was all over, and I opened my eyes, it was after 4 a.m. Yet it seemed as if it had been only 10 or 15 minutes.)

The Lord spoke to me. Among other things, He gave me

instructions concerning the Prayer and Healing School we are now holding every weekday on the RHEMA Bible Training Center campus.

And I saw something. I saw three things coming up out of the Atlantic Ocean. They looked like three giant black frogs as large as whales. One was in midair. The other two had just stuck their heads up out of the water from the east.

I had seen something similar nine years before.

Jesus said to me, "You saw the same thing in 1970. I told you then exactly what they were, but you didn't do what you should have done about it. I told you back in 1970 to pray for the leaders of the nation. What happened [Watergate and so forth] isn't all the fault of the man who was then President. I am going to hold the Christians of this nation responsible. You are the ones who allowed what happened to your nation. If you had prayed, it never would have happened. I showed you what was about to happen. Go back and check . . . . "

(Later, I went back and checked what the Lord had said to me in 1970 from tapes and manuscripts of a special meeting we held in October 1970.)

Jesus said to me, "Back in 1970, you saw three similar dark objects come up out of the Atlantic and leapfrog all the way across the land. If you and the Christians had done what you should have done, none of those things would have happened to your nation. You would not have had the riots. You would not have had the political disturbances. Your President would not have made the mistakes he made. In fact, I am holding the Church responsible for his mistakes."

I began to weep and cry, "Oh, God!"

"Yes," He said, "I am holding you and the Church

responsible."

Then He said, "When you tell that to some of the Christians, they will laugh. But when they stand before my judgment seat and they receive the condemnation rather than the man who was then President, they won't laugh.

"If Christians had done what I told them to do in the Bible—if they had prayed for the leaders of their nation— they would have kept the evil spirits from operating."

Then He continued, "Similar things—not the same things—but similar things are about to happen again. If you do not pray, they will happen. I am not going to hold the President responsible for the nation; I am going to hold the Christians of the nation responsible."

Now, let me explain something—you have to know how to interpret these things. I saw those three creatures come up out of the Atlantic Ocean. But that doesn't mean they rise out of the ocean. From Genesis to Revelation "seas" and "waters" refer to a multitude of people. Out of the multitude of people, these things will rise up. Sinners are dominated by the devil; they're in his kingdom.

Jesus said, "There will arise, unless the Christians pray, not for the same purpose that the other riots came— but there will be riots, tumults, and disturbances all across the nation.

"Second, something is about to happen to the President that should not happen—and will not happen if you will pray.

"Third, something is about to happen again that will bring further trouble in the economic scene, the financial structure.

"But you can stop all three. You can stop the upheaval in the social structure. You can stop the upheaval and the

activity of the devil in the political scene. You can stop the devil from disrupting the financial scene of your nation.

"You can change all three through intercessory prayer. That's one of the main purposes for the classes you are going to start in the fall."

First Things First

God gave us specific instructions to put first things first.

"Yes, but," people have said to me, "I'll tell you, as long as the Democrats are in, it's not going to go." Others have said, "As long as the Republicans are in . . . . "

If you are party minded first, you will never amount to much of a Christian. Christians are to put first things first.

The Word says, *"I exhort therefore, that, first of all . . . . "*

First! Before you pray for your children, before you pray for me, before I pray for you, *" . . . first of all, supplications, prayers, intercessions, and giving of thanks, be made for all men; For kings, and for all that are in authority . . . . "*

So we would know who the "all men" are, it says, *"For kings, and for all that are in authority."*

First of all, we are to pray for our leaders—for all those who are in authority in national government, state or provincial government, and on down to city government.

Why? Go on reading . . . .

" . . . that we may lead a quiet and peaceable life in all godliness and honesty . . . . " That "we" as Christians may lead a quiet and peaceable life. God is interested in us.

All the kings Paul was instructing them to pray for were not born again.

Will God bless leaders even though they are not saved?

Certainly. The Spirit of God would not tell us to pray for something we could not have. That would be stupid.

Why will He bless them? For one thing, He is interested in us.

"For this is good and acceptable in the sight of God our Saviour . . . ." It is good and acceptable in the sight of God our Savior that we pray first of all for all who are in authority. It is good and acceptable in the sight of God our Savior that we lead a quiet and peaceable life.

"Who will have all men to be saved, and to come unto the knowledge of the truth." When there is war—when there is upheaval—when there is turmoil—it is difficult to spread the Gospel. But when there is peace—when there is tranquility—then we are free to go and spread the Gospel.

No wonder the devil wants to attack the United States, for instance. You can go around the world and you will find that 90 percent of all missionary work is done from America. If the devil could stop us, he could stop the flow of God's blessings.

But, blessed be God, he cannot do it!

How are we told to pray for those in authority?

" . . . supplications, prayers, intercessions, and giving of thanks . . . ."

The prayer of intercession is a prayer for others. This Scripture is talking about praying for others—for those who are in authority. An intercessor takes the place of another, or pleads another's case.

One Bible example is Abraham's intercession for two cities—Sodom and Gomorrah. Read that account in Genesis chapter 18.

The Lord said, *"Shall I hide from Abraham that thing which I do"* (v. 17).

He would not destroy those wicked cities without

informing His blood-covenant friend.

Abraham was standing on his blood-covenant rights when he said to the Lord, *"Wilt thou also destroy the righteous with the wicked? Peradventure there be fifty righteous within the city: wilt thou also destroy and not spare the place for the fifty righteous that are therein? That be far from thee to do after this manner, to slay the righteous with the wicked: and that the righteous should be as the wicked, that be far from thee: Shall not the Judge of all the earth do right?* (vv. 23-25).

The Lord said, *"If I find in Sodom fifty righteous within the city, then I will spare the place for THEIR sakes"* (v. 26).

Remember what First Timothy 2:2 said, *" . . . that WE may lead a quiet and peaceable life . . . . "*?

God said He would spare the whole city for the sake of 50 righteous.

Abraham kept going down in number until he said to the Lord, *"Peradventure ten shall be found there."*

And the Lord said, *"I will not destroy it for ten's sake"* (v. 32).

Consider the terrible sins that existed in Sodom—yet God said He would spare the whole place for ten's sake.

You know, this old world would already have been destroyed if it were not for us Christians. Jesus said, *"Ye are the salt of the earth"* (Matt. 5:13).

I am old enough to remember before we had electric refrigerators. My grandfather killed hogs. He'd put salt on the meat to preserve it.

This world is bad enough—but if it were not for us Christians, it would certainly be rotten.

God told Abraham He would spare the cities for the sake of ten righteous. There are more than ten righteous persons in America today.

Some say, "We're going to pot."

No, we're not!

Don't listen to such talk as that.

I believe there are people in America today who will take their place in prayer just as Abraham did.

Abraham didn't sit around and talk about how wicked they were and how they were all going to hell. *He interceded on their behalf!*

If we will take our place, we can change things.

We have a better covenant based on better promises!

I was in the home of a minister of the Gospel whose 4-year-old son was so misbehaved he embarrassed me, and even embarrassed my son, who was also 4. Ken said to me the minute we got into the car, "That boy is awful, isn't he?"

He talked terribly to his father. When his father picked him up in his arms, petting him a little to quieten him down, the boy slapped his cheeks and said, "You old liar. What you're telling is not so. You're a liar."

This pastor—Full Gospel, Spirit-filled—said to me, "Well, you know, the Bible says that in the last days, children will be disobedient to parents."

"Yes," I said, "the Bible also says that the love of many shall wax cold, but that doesn't mean my love has to wax cold. And that doesn't mean my children are going to be disobedient to their parents."

You can sit around and say, "Well, the Bible says that evil men and seducers will wax worse and worse, deceived and being deceived. This whole thing is going down. The love of many shall wax cold," and if you just dwell on that side, you will grow cold. The devil will take you over and all your children.

But, you don't have to think along that line.

Wake up and realize who you are in Christ. The gates of hell shall not prevail against the Church! Jesus is the Head of the Church—not Satan. Jesus is bigger than the devil. In fact, He already has defeated him. He arose victorious over him—and His victory is my victory.

Think in line with God's Word and realize that no matter what the situation, we can do something about it.

> **EZEKIEL 22:30,31**
> **30 And I sought for a man among them, that should make up the hedge, and stand in the gap before me for the land, that I should not destroy it: but I found none.**
> **31 Therefore have I poured out mine indignation upon them; I have consumed them with the fire of my wrath: their own way have I recompensed upon their heads.**

This is God talking. Abraham interceded for two cities. Here God is talking about an entire nation. If He could have found ONE man who would have stood in the gap, who would have interceded on behalf of the nation, judgment would not have come.

"Well," someone might ask, "if God really wanted to spare the land, why didn't He just go ahead and do it anyhow? Isn't He God? If that's His will, why doesn't He go ahead and do it?"

Go back to First Timothy 2:4. There it says that God wills that all men come unto the knowledge of the truth. Why doesn't He just go ahead and make them all be born again? If He can do anything He wants to do, why doesn't He do it? Why does He wait for somebody to intercede?

We discussed this in detail in Chapter One, "Why Pray?"

Satan became the god of this world until Adam's lease runs out. He is not my god—I am not of this world. But he is responsible for the wars between nations, the murders, the violence that is done in the world.

God will not transgress His own Word. He gave the lease to Adam. Adam gave it to the devil. It is running out. But until that time, God can only intervene as Christians seek His face and ask Him to move.

Satan's authority over matters on the earth can only be overcome as Christians pray and intercede in the behalf of their country. God is longing today for someone who will make up the hedge and stand in the gap before Him for the land.

Intercession can be made in your known tongue. It can best be made in other tongues as the Holy Spirit helps you to make intercession. Ask the Holy Spirit to help you, and *continue* to make intercession.

Here is where some people miss it. They don't hear everything you teach, and they grab some little something and run off with it. There are some things you can pray the prayer of faith on—and you pray one prayer and that's the end of it. You don't have to pray anymore; you just thank God for the answer. You can do that for salvation, for the baptism in the Holy Spirit, for healing—for anything God promised right now. But there are other things you cannot pray the prayer of faith on. One of them is this scene we are talking about—*continue* to pray the prayer of intercession for the leaders of your nation.

Chapter 28

Reviving the Art

The art of intercession has been virtually lost in the Church. Early-day Pentecostals knew something about it. Second-generation Pentecostals knew a little about it. Third-generation Pentecostals know almost nothing about it. Charismatics know almost nothing about it.

But for God to accomplish what He desires to accomplish in the '80s, the art of intercessory prayer will have to be resurrected.

When I first received the baptism in the Holy Spirit and came over among Pentecostal people, I accepted the pastorate of a small Full Gospel church in the black land of North Central Texas. Most of the congregation were farmers.

In the fall of the year when they harvested cotton, we dismissed all services except for Saturday night, Sunday morning, and Sunday night. On Sunday afternoons, we'd bring something to eat and gather at someone's house to eat together.

This particular Sunday we met at my future wife's house. A dear little lady was there. I had heard of her, but had never met her. Everyone called her Mother Howard. They referred to her as "a mother in Israel."

She ate. But as soon as we finished eating, and were visiting, she asked for a room where she could get off by herself. She knelt on the bare floor. (I learned that sometimes she would put a newspaper on the floor and lay her forehead on it as she prayed all Sunday afternoon without moving.)

She was a widow. She owned her own home in a neighboring community. A pastor I knew lived in one side of her home with his wife and child.

He said to me, "She makes a business of prayer. She arises at 4 in the morning. She prays from 4 to 8 every morning. Then she cooks her a little bite to eat. After that she puts in another two hours praying. She eats a light lunch, then she usually comes over to our side of the house and visits with us a while. By 2 or 3 in the afternoon she goes back to prayer. Sometimes she prays until midnight. If the burden is there, she prays all night."

Hers was a ministry of intercession.

She was born again many years ago in Dallas. Then they had moved to a town where there was no Full Gospel church. In fact, there was no Full Gospel church in any city or town around about.

One by one, town by town, city by city, she took them, and interceded until a church was built there. Then she took the next town, and prayed until a church was built there.

Mother Howard, that little old woman, that beautiful saint of God, prayed a church into every town, every village, and every nook of North Texas.

I've thought about how it might be when we all get to Heaven and the rewards are passed out. The pastors who built the churches will be ready to step up and get their reward, but Jesus is going to call Mother Howard up there!

Hers was the ministry that got the job done! No one saw her. They hardly knew she existed. But she didn't wile her time visiting and talking on Sunday afternoons. She was on the job. She literally gave her life for others.

That's what Jesus did. And He is calling for intercessors today.

Chapter 29

Excesses

In the Bible, particularly in Old Testament times, people were set apart or consecrated to a sacred office by the anointing of oil. Oil was a type of the Holy Spirit. The Holy Spirit would come upon men and women to anoint them to stand in a particular office. In the New Testament, God is still anointing His people. Not everyone in the Body of Christ is called and anointed of God to one of the five-fold ministry gifts. But every Christian is called and anointed of God to reign and rule as a king and priest in this life.

> **REVELATION 1:6**
> 6 And [God] hath made us kings and priests unto God and his Father; to him be glory and dominion for ever and ever. Amen.
>
> **REVELATION 5:10**
> 10 And [God] has made us unto our God kings and priests: and we shall reign on the earth.

When you think about priests, you immediately think about intercession. The priest is a "go-between"; one who prays to God on behalf of people, and that's where intercession comes in. You don't pray the prayer of intercession for yourself. An intercessor goes into the presence of God for those who are hindered in going to God, or for those who don't know they can go to God themselves.

We must remember that the devil thrives on ignorance. Ignorant of God's Word, some Christians fall into the error of spiritual pride, thinking: *We're a special class of people. We have a special ministry, and a special calling; no one else is like us.* That's exactly what the devil wants. That's the same way he sinned. Lucifer was lifted up in pride.

Instead of getting elevated about it, we need to take the attitude: Thank God, we are all anointed to be priests; let's get after it!

> 1 PETER 2:5,9
> 5   Ye also, as lively stones, are built up a spiritual house, an holy priesthood [that's all of us; the whole Body of Christ!], to offer up spiritual sacrifices, acceptable to God by Jesus Christ.
> 9   But ye are a chosen generation, a royal priesthood, an holy nation, a peculiar people; that ye should shew forth the praises of him who hath called you out of darkness into his marvellous light.

You see how far people can get off on some of these issues. Actually, intercession is not a *special* calling— everyone in the Body of Christ is to be an intercessor because God has anointed every one of us to be priests unto our God. The whole Body of Christ has been called out of darkness into light and is a part of this royal priesthood, not just a *chosen few.* Some have responded more readily to the Holy Spirit and entered into it more than others, but intercession belongs to every born-again Christian.

Because people think they have some *special calling,* they think they have to *perform.* So they try to do something in the flesh instead of waiting on the anointing. People get off into error when they take spiritual things out of context. Some are even going around saying they stand in the "office of the intercessor." They say this "office" puts them on the same level as the minister or pastor, so that gives them the right to tell the pastor what to do! In the first place, there is no such thing as the "office" of intercessor. We find the five-fold offices or ministry gifts which *God set in the Church,* listed in

Ephesians 4:11,12:

> **EPHESIANS 4:11,12**
> 11 And he gave some, apostles; and some, prophets; and
> some, evangelists; and some, pastors and teachers;
> 12 For the perfecting of the saints, for the work of the
> ministry, for the edifying of the body of Christ.

We can readily see that intercession is not mentioned
here in Ephesians. That's because intercession is not a
ministry gift. We need to keep spiritual matters in their
rightful place, and not get them out of place. Also, we need
to clarify what we mean when we say that intercession
is a *ministry*. If we are using the word "ministry" in a
general sense, that's one thing. Generally speaking,
anything you do for God is a ministry. In that case,
intercession could be considered as a *ministry,* just as
anything we do for God is a ministry—a service—unto
God. But if we are speaking specifically, using the word
"ministry" as one of the five-fold ministry gifts given to
the Church, then, no, intercession is not a *ministry.*
Intercession is not a ministry gift.

> **1 CORINTHIANS 12:28**
> 28 And God hath set some in the church, first apostles,
> secondarily prophets, thirdly teachers, after that miracles,
> then gifts of healings, HELPS, governments, diversities
> of tongues.

If we are using "ministry" in a general sense, then
intercession would have to come under the ministry of
helps. The saints are not perfected through intercession.
Yes, we can pray for people, help and bless them, but that
doesn't *perfect* them. Ephesians 4:11,12 says that the
offices of the apostle, prophet, evangelist, pastor, and

teacher are for the *perfecting* of the saints. If it took intercession to perfect the saints, the Bible would have mentioned intercession as a ministry gift. No, intercession *helps* people.

Secondly, the ministry of helps is not on the same level as the five-fold ministry gifts. The ministry of helps includes anything that helps or assists those in the five-fold ministry function as they should.

Intercession With Groanings

ROMANS 8:26
26 Likewise the Spirit also helpeth our infirmities: for we know not what we should pray for as we ought: but the Spirit itself [Himself] maketh intercession for us with groanings which cannot be uttered.

Another excess that has arisen in intercession, is this issue of *groanings*. Many times people try to carry out spiritual things in the natural and in the flesh. God *anoints* His people to carry out His will and purposes, but when people get over into the flesh, they get into trouble. It's one thing to groan under the anointing of the Holy Spirit. But on the other hand, you can do all the groaning in the flesh you want to, but without the anointing you are not going to produce anything. When the Holy Spirit moves on you to "make intercession with groanings which cannot be uttered," there will be results! The problem is people are trying to mimic and imitate the Holy Spirit and they get off into error.

Questions and Answers

Some have asked, "Is it possible to groan in the Spirit

as an act of the will?'' There's no Scripture for groaning
as an act of the will. The Bible says, "*... the Spirit itself*
[Himself] *maketh intercession for us with groanings ...*"
(Rom. 8:26). Sometimes people just naturally groan
because they are burdened, and it's not the Holy Spirit
at all. But it's another thing when the Spirit takes hold.
I've found that praising and worshipping God many times
leads into this realm where the Spirit of God begins to take
hold together with your spirit in groanings. But you can't
just do it yourself—that's the point I'm trying to get over
to you.

   People ask, "Can a person travail as an act of the will?"
Paul said in Galatians 4:19: *"My little children, of whom
I travail in birth again until Christ be formed in you."* Paul
uses the same term as a woman in travail to birth a child.
Can a woman travail as an act of her will? No! If there's
no child to bring forth, she could try to travail but nothing
would come of it. The Spirit of God brings us into travail
because He knows there's something there to give birth
to. For example, some people are saved because they hear
the Word of God and believe it. But there are others who
will never be saved unless someone travails for them. We
don't know who they are; only the Spirit of God knows.

   Can you travail to birth something anytime you want?
Well, could a woman give birth to a baby anytime she
wants? No, she has to be pregnant first. Can travail be
loosed upon people by the laying on of hands? No, that's
laying empty hands on empty heads. Is groaning more
effective than praying in tongues? Certainly not. So much
of what we do, if we're not careful, is in the flesh! And
sometimes it is a mixture of the two.

   Of course you can stir yourself up in prayer at any time.
And there is a wrestling in prayer that takes strenuous

effort (Eph. 6:12). Daniel stirred himself up to pray and wrestled in prayer. I've stirred myself up to seek God, and then the Holy Spirit took hold with me. And we do have a scriptural basis for this because the Word of God says, *"Stir up the gift of God, which is in thee . . ."* (2 Tim. 1:6).

Is there a difference between travailing and wrestling? Certainly there is a difference. Travail is a term used of a woman travailing in birth. Paul said, *". . .I travail in birth again until Christ be formed in you"* (Gal. 4:19). Wrestling is wrestling against the forces of evil.

We need to remember that we need all kinds of praying, not just one kind. Don't misunderstand me; thank God for intercession. But the Bible says, *"Praying always with all prayer"* (Eph. 6:18), or as one translation says, "Praying with all kinds of prayer." So we need all kinds of prayer. Let's learn to be sensitive to the Holy Spirit, and see which way He is moving at the moment and what direction He wants to take. Then let's just follow Him!